AMERICAN ACCENT DRILLS FOR BRITISH AND AUSTRALIAN SPEAKERS

American Accent Drills for British and Australian Speakers provides a comprehensive guide to learning a "General American" accent, made specifically for native English speakers.

Unlike most American accent guides, which are geared toward ESL learners, this handbook covers only the shifts that English speakers need to make – nothing more, nothing less. In addition to vowel and consonant drills, it covers the finer points of American intonation and elision, features that often elude English speakers of other dialects. Finally, it provides exercises for "owning" the dialect, finding authenticity and making it work for each individual actor in their own way.

This is an excellent resource for students of speech and dialects, actors from the UK, Australia, and New Zealand, and advanced ESL learners who need to use an American accent on screen or on stage.

American Accent Drills for British and Australian Speakers also includes access to downloadable audio files of the practice drills featured in the book, to help students practice and perfect their American accent.

Amanda Quaid has over 15 years of experience teaching speech, dialects, and language skills to actors and other speakers from around the world. In addition to her coaching on plays, films, and television, she maintains a thriving private practice in New York City. She is on faculty at the New School and HB Studio, both in New York City, and has been featured as a dialect expert on WNYC.

AMERICAN ACCENT DRILLS FOR BRITISH AND AUSTRALIAN SPEAKERS

Amanda Quaid

NEW YORK AND LONDON

First published 2020
by Routledge
52 Vanderbilt Avenue, New York, NY 10017

and by Routledge
2 Park Square, Milton Park, Abingdon, Oxon, OX14 4RN

Routledge is an imprint of the Taylor & Francis Group, an informa business

© 2020 Amanda Quaid

The right of Amanda Quaid to be identified as author of this work has been asserted by her in accordance with sections 77 and 78 of the Copyright, Designs and Patents Act 1988.

All rights reserved. No part of this book may be reprinted or reproduced or utilised in any form or by any electronic, mechanical, or other means, now known or hereafter invented, including photocopying and recording, or in any information storage or retrieval system, without permission in writing from the publishers.

Trademark notice: Product or corporate names may be trademarks or registered trademarks, and are used only for identification and explanation without intent to infringe.

Library of Congress Cataloging-in-Publication Data
Names: Quaid, Amanda, author.
Title: American accent drills for British and Australian speakers / Amanda Quaid.
Description: New York, NY : Routledge, 2020. | Includes index.
Identifiers: LCCN 2019049356 (print) | LCCN 2019049357 (ebook) | ISBN 9780367365646 (hardback) | ISBN 9780367365653 (paperback) | ISBN 9780429347122 (ebook)
Subjects: LCSH: English language–United States–Pronunciation by foreign speakers. | English language–Spoken English–United States–Problems, exercises, etc.
Classification: LCC PE2815 .Q33 2020 (print) | LCC PE2815 (ebook) | DDC 421/.52071–dc23
LC record available at https://lccn.loc.gov/2019049356
LC ebook record available at https://lccn.loc.gov/2019049357

ISBN: 978-0-3673-6564-6 (hbk)
ISBN: 978-0-3673-6565-3 (pbk)
ISBN: 978-0-429-34712-2 (ebk)

Typeset in Bembo
by Swales & Willis, Exeter, Devon, UK

Visit the eResources: www.routledge.com/9780367365653

Dedicated to the original GenAm Gym.
Thank you for your inspiration, courage, and humor.

CONTENTS

Preface: The GenAm Gym   *x*
Acknowledgements   *xii*

Introduction   1
A "General American" Accent? 1
Who Is This Book For? 2
For Actors in the US: Added Pressure 3
How to Use This Book 4
How to Use the Audio Guide 5
For Instructors 5

1   Vowels and Diphthongs   7
Articulators 7
[æ] as in Trap *and* Bath   *9*
[a:] as in Thought, Lot, *and* Palm   *12*
[i:] as in Fleece   *17*
[u:] as in Goose   *19*
[ʌ] as in Strut   *22*

viii Contents

> *[oŭ] as in* Goat 25
> *[eĭ] as in* Face 27
> *[aĭ] as in* Price 29
> *[aŭ] as in* Mouth 31

2 T and L — 33

Introduction to T 33
Voiced [t] 33
Special Topic: To 34
Glottalized T [ʔ] 36
Held [t̚] 38
Vanishing [t] 40
Introduction to L 41

3 R — 43

Introduction to R 43
[ɝː] as in Nurse 45
[ɚ] as in Letter 48
[ɪɚ] as in Near 50
[ɛɚ] as in Square 52
[ɔɚ] as in Force 54
[aɚ] as in Start 57
R to TH 59
Intrusive R 60
Fluffy Suffixes 61

4 Elision — 63

I'm Going To 63
Why Don't You/Let Me/Trying To 65
Is This/Is That/Is There and Was This/Was That/Was There 66
It's/That's 68
Should We? Could We? Can We? 69
Can't You? Won't You? Don't You? 70
Did You? Could You? Would You? Should You? 71

5 Challenging Words 73
What, From, Of 73
Was/Wasn't 75
Actually 76
Something 77

6 Intonation and Identity 79
Introduction to GenAm Intonation 79
Question Intonation 81
Valley Girls and Surfer Dudes 82
Accent as Identity 82
What Are Your Stereotypes? 83
"When I Speak This Way …" 83
"Where Are You From?" 85
Refining Your GenAm 86

Appendix In Their Own Words: Actors on Acting in GenAm **91**

PREFACE: THE GENAM GYM

I'd been coaching accents in New York City for about 10 years when I suddenly had an influx of British clients who wanted a "General American" accent (also known as GenAm). At first, I thought the goals of these actors would be similar to those of my French, Russian, and Japanese clients. I used the same practice material and the same approach. And while we made progress, it soon became clear that these actors faced challenges all their own.

For one thing, they (obviously) spoke English natively. They weren't trying to sound clearer in a foreign language, they were changing the sounds of their mother tongue. Many were dismayed that, though they had a clear advantage over a foreign-language speaker, they were still unable to "get it". We dug deeper, and I asked them to describe their feelings about doing this work in the first place. That's where it got interesting.

Nearly all had strong feelings of ambivalence about speaking in an American accent. Some felt they were "selling out." Some even felt they were betraying their families. Nearly all of them felt less intelligent in GenAm. Even those who could nail the accent were terribly self-conscious. It was as if their identity had been erased, their charm, their origin story. Suddenly they were all ironed out—sounding perfectly

American, but bland. They felt so much of their focus was on the accent that paralysis set in when they began to act. And they felt isolated.

So, I started a class just for them, which we called the GenAm Gym. Each week, we gathered together for 2 hours and worked on a specific aspect of the accent. We also worked on monologues, scenes, and on-camera improv. We did mock interviews. We practiced talking about our origin stories using an American accent. Every exercise I could think of, I threw at them, and they were game.

After a month or so, they started half-jokingly referring to the Gym as "group therapy," and indeed it did take on a certain therapeutic quality. They shared tales of auditions gone wrong, they told stories of being asked to do their American accent at parties and having well-meaning friends make fun of them, they laughed and cried. They commiserated about the dreaded question, "Where are you from?" And, most of all, they celebrated each other's triumphs. When someone booked a role requiring an American accent (which began to happen more and more), we all cheered and worked on the scenes as a group.

I dedicate this book to them, because it was through that class that I began to see accent work as a whole-person endeavor. You can't just work the sounds, you need to work the mind. And you need support. This guide is designed to be your teacher, ally, and companion through your GenAm journey, to bring you as close as possible to that feeling of being part of the Gym. It's my honor to accompany you. I hope you find what you're looking for here.

ACKNOWLEDGEMENTS

First and foremost, I'd like to acknowledge the GenAm Gym members Michael Dale, Lisa Donmall-Reeve, Lily Dorment, Mark Evans, Richard Hollis, Laura Hooper, Curt James, Sarah Manton, Polly McKie, Charles Nassif, Olivia Phillip, James Rees, Robert Spence, Scarlett Strallen, and Oliver Thornton. Their talent, generosity, and support made this book possible.

Thanks also to Scott Miller and John Patrick, who peer-reviewed this material and provided great insights and mentorship. To Jan Gist, who introduced me to the core principles of accent-as-identity work. And thanks to Susan Patrick for her teaching and encouragement.

Thanks to Stacey Walker and Lucia Accorsi at Routledge, and my editor, Sonnie Wills, for guidance and support.

And thanks always to Noel and Alma.

INTRODUCTION

A "General American" Accent?

So-called "General American" (GenAm) is a dialect that sounds distinctly American, but not regionally specific. In other words, it ensures intelligibility across the United States, but doesn't place you in Brooklyn, Fargo, or Tallahassee. It's educated, but not fussy; casual, but not sloppy.

The reason I refer to it as *so-called* "General American" is that the term falls into a hierarchy I don't subscribe to. Historically, dialects associated with Caucasian, middle-class speakers are said to be "general," much in the way the plummy vowels of England's upper classes are acquired if one wishes to be "received" in those groups. It's a flawed construct with a troubling social history.

So, I'm not here to tell you this is the "right" way to speak. It's a jumping-off point, a roadmap to get you in the ballpark. I suggest you learn this "general" dialect as a base, and then, using native speaker models, refine it to what works for you, perhaps based on your ethnicity, age, and gender. Chapter 6 lists suggestions for honing your specific American sound.

Also, I urge you not to think of this work as "accent reduction." You may have picked up this book at the suggestion of your agent or teacher, who may have told you to "reduce" your accent. While well-meaning, it's not a helpful mindset. What you're doing is **accent acquisition**. You are *adding* an American accent to your arsenal, not annihilating your own. My goal for you is to **code-switch** with ease, dropping into American when

> **Code-switching** is going back and forth between different ways of speaking in order to fit in with various groups. We all do it, to some degree. Ask yourself, how do I already speak differently to different people?

you need to, and going right back to your native accent when you wish.

Who Is This Book For?

There is currently no book on the market designed specifically for native English speakers who want to learn an American accent. Generally, you'll find "accent reduction" texts, hefty guides with drills that may or may not pertain to you.

So, if you speak English natively and are looking for a guide, this is for you. While it is targeted mainly to actors from the UK and Australia, it would also be suitable for speakers from Ireland, New Zealand, and Canada. It's also suitable for ESL speakers who are quite far along with their American accent training and want to fine-tune their sound or get to the next level of proficiency.

Please be advised, this book lays out my best understanding of how *laypeople* speak in America at this moment. It's how someone would sound if you stopped them in the street. It's not the sound of an actor who attended drama school and learned "good speech." So, if you are a student in a program with a speech instructor, a lot of what we cover may directly contradict what your teacher has told you to do. It may even feel "sloppy" by comparison. That's okay! Remember, this dialect is not a "standard." It's one sound among many you may be called upon to use as an actor. Treat it as a tool and not an end point in your speech training.

For Actors in the US: Added Pressure

If you're a British or Australian actor working in America, you face additional pressure. It's one thing to do an American accent for other Brits in Manchester. It's another to do it in New York. The clients who come to me are often baffled by a kind of primal fear that kicks in when they do their American accent for other Americans. They sweat. Their voices shake. They turn red. Why?

Because accents are tribal. Humans have accents in order to tell, immediately, who is an insider or an outsider to their group. In the Bible, a tribe used a single word, *shibboleth*, as a test to see who belonged with them. They pronounced it with a "sh" sound, but a neighboring tribe pronounced it with "s." To catch imposters, they gave them a test: say this word. If you pronounced it correctly, you were let in. If you didn't, well ... they killed you!

No doubt about it—accents can be scary. Nobody's going to kill you, of course, but on some primal level, you may fear that they will. That anxiety has a foundation deep in your unconscious.

Let's see how that might play out in an everyday scenario. Imagine you're on your way to an audition in America, to play an American character. You debated with yourself whether to speak in an American accent from the beginning of the audition, trying to "pass" as American. After all, won't that be less distracting than switching from your native accent into your American? But you second-guess yourself. You remember all the times Americans told you they love your native accent. What if your accent is the most appealing thing about you?

This inner dialogue continues as you enter the building and sign in. You give your name to the desk attendant and don't recognize the voice that comes out of your mouth. Did that sound American? Or did it just sound weird? The waiting room is full of American actors. Actors who don't have to go in thinking about how they sound. Not you. You were up all night going over not only your acting choices, but also your vowels. And you're still not sure about every single word.

The casting director calls your name. You have to make a choice. American. You'll go in American and see how it goes. You enter the room. After you slate, the casting director asks the dreaded question: "Where are you from?" Even worse, she follows it up with "I hear a little bit of an accent." You smile and, through gritted teeth, confess your true nationality. She asks, "Can you do the sides in an American accent?" You resist the urge to shout, "*This is my American accent!*"

You do the scene and feel tight, self-conscious, and defeated. Worse than that, you feel exposed and fraudulent. Does this scenario sound familiar? You're not alone. With practice bravely putting your accent out in the world, you will start to feel more confident.

How to Use This Book

I use symbols from the International Phonetic Alphabet (IPA) throughout, to be as clear as possible about variations which may be quite subtle. If you don't know the IPA, or it gives you hives, that's fine. You can click and hear the symbols at www.ipachart.com, or simply rely on the audio guide and make your own notes.

Symbols from the IPA appear in brackets, such as [b]. When I refer to a letter used in English spelling, that letter appears between slash marks, such as/b/. In other words, the word *thumb* contains a spelled/b/, but not a spoken [b]. (I occasionally break this rule for the sake of simplicity.)

Try to identify if you are primarily an *aural, visual,* or *kinesthetic learner.* This will help you work through the book in the manner best suited to your learning style. Aural learners pick things up *by ear,* so the audio is your best guide. Visual learners need to *see* it. Use the phonetic alphabet or your own "faux-netic" alphabet that makes sense to you—but by all means, write things down. Kinesthetic learners need to *feel.* You'll rely most heavily on the descriptions of the placement of your tongue, lips, and jaw.

Each chapter gives you a description of the sound, followed by samples of words, phrases, and sentences. You'll find "How do I say ... ?" boxes with special pronunciations of challenging words. There are also "Scramblers" throughout, which put tricky sounds side-by-side for an extra challenge. Some chapters include dialogues you can do with a friend to practice conversation. Work through these at your own pace, with the audio, and be sure to apply what you're learning to text on a regular basis. No need to go in order—if you want to head straight to Chapter 3 for exmaple, that's a-okay. Be sure to visit the Appendix for words of wisdom from fellow actors who have put this work into practice.

How to Use the Audio Guide

The audio files accompanying this book are available for download at routledge.com. Visit www.routledge.com/9780367365653 and click the eResources tab.

For Instructors

This is meant to be a highly accessible guide to a casual GenAm sound. Much of what I describe is not widely accepted as standard speech and may be controversial. Some of this I include because I want to be accurate about what laypeople actually say (e.g. a nasal diphthong in *can* and *ham*), and some because I've found Brits and Aussies are more likely to hit the target sound if they approach it this way (e.g. a *thought*, *lot* and *palm* merger). I also err on the side of strong r-coloring (see Chapter 3), which I know may not be right for all speakers or performance circumstances. I urge you to adapt the exercises to suit both your students and your personal style.

1
VOWELS AND DIPHTHONGS

Articulators

Before we launch into our first sound, let's explore the parts of your anatomy you use to make speech, your **articulators**. You have many articulators, but these are the ones we'll reference in this book.

Immovable Articulators

Teeth: the upper teeth are used for the consonant sounds [θ] as in *three,* [ð] as in *them*, [f] as in *five,* and [v] as in *vine.* The lower serve as an anchor point for the tongue when it shapes vowel sounds.
Gum ridge: the bump behind your upper teeth (also called the **alveolar ridge**). Used for articulating [t] as in *time*, [d] as in *dime*, [n] as in *no,* [l] as in *love,* and as a reference area for the GenAm R sound (also see Chapter 3).
Hard palate: the "roof of your mouth."

Moveable Articulators

Lips: can be rounded, neutral, or retracted. Lip corners can protrude, stay neutral or pull back.

8 Vowels and Diphthongs

Tongue: cups down or arches up in the front, middle, and back for vowel shaping. To feel the movement of the tongue, try saying "ee—aw—ee—aw" without moving your jaw. You should feel an undulation, front to back. The tongue also articulates various consonant sounds.

Tip of tongue: the very front point, used to articulate [t], [d], [n], [l], [θ], [ð], and the GenAm R sound.

Blade of tongue: the area right behind the tip of the tongue.

Soft palate: behind the hard palate, the soft palate raises when you yawn and lowers when you say a word like "sing." (Also called the **velum**.)

Jaw: raises up and lowers down for vowel shaping.

Glottis: the open space between your vocal folds. When the folds come together to close the glottis, as when you cough, you'll experience a little "pop" in your airflow. To feel it at work, say "uh oh!"

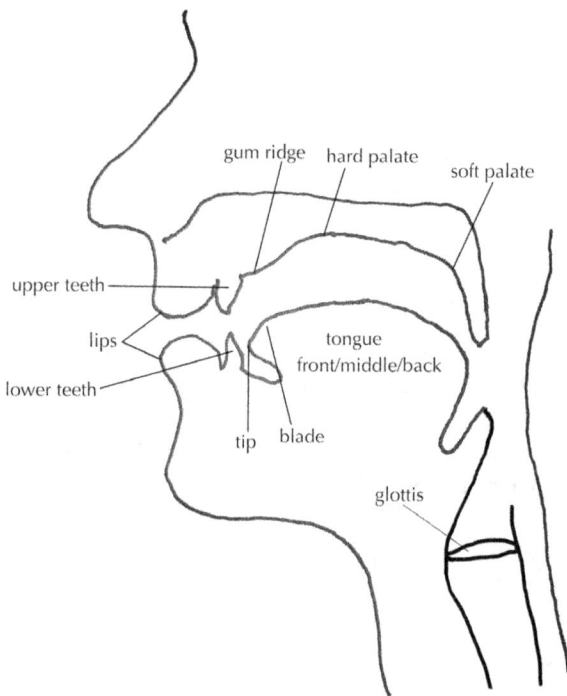

FIGURE 1.1 Articulators

[æ] as in *Trap* and *Bath*

This is a sound I like to start with because it requires some boldness. It's that brassy, sometimes nasal sound Brits and Aussies tend to dislike in American speech. Jump in and go for it, using the audio as a guide. If you go too far at first, it's easy to pull back.

Structure

Tongue: tip touches the lower front teeth, and front of tongue cups down.
Lips: retracted (slight smile).
Jaw: released and may be ever-so-slightly lowered.

Words

1. apple   cap   gap   lap   map   nap   perhaps   tap   cab   crab   fabulous   bat   cat   fat   rat   sat   Saturday   bad   dad   glad   mad   sad   sadly   back   Jack   lack   pack   quack   rack   sack   vacuum   bag   tag   flag   gag   Africa   traffic   avenue   average   lavender   savage   Al   pal   athlete   Katherine   math   fascinate   passenger   gas   ash   cash   crash   dash   mash   rash   trash   badge   imagine   pack   lack   lad   gladly   status
2. after   bath   path   ask   disaster   grass   pass   class   fast   cast   last   giraffe   master   laugh   basket   blasted   craft   nasty   mask   pasture   pass   raspberry   half
3. (note: these might sound a bit more nasal—see the upcoming Special Topic)   advantage   answer   can't   chance   dance   enhance   France   plant   example   reprimand   command   grant
4. (note: the stress falls on the second syllable)   caffeine   café

Phrases

1. sad, glad or mad?
2. trash bag
3. fascinating class
4. relaxing bath
5. Katherine's passions
6. vacuum bag
7. fat cat
8. Jack's values
9. pass the basket
10. bad traffic
11. Madison Avenue
12. last laugh

Vowels and Diphthongs

Sentences

1. The actress gave a class on craft.
2. Jack chatted out back with Katherine.
3. The giraffes in Africa were commanding.
4. I'm asking Alice to answer, not Al.
5. Their nasty laughter made dad sad.
6. Matt had a relaxing bath on Saturday.

Special Topic: [æ] + [n], [m], [ŋ]

Before the nasal consonants [n] as in *can*, [m] as in *ham,* and [ŋ] as in *hang,* the vowel may become diphthongized (drawn out) and nasalized (given a quality of nasality). Note that the vowel before [n] and [m] is the same, but different before [ŋ].

[ɛ̃ən]	*[ɛ̃əm]*	*[ɛ̃ɪŋ]*
can't	camera	canker
ban	bam	bank
Anna	amber	angle
Dan	damp	dangle
fan	family	fang
began	gamma	gang
can	camp	kangaroo
pan	Pamela	pancreatic
hand	ham	hang
January	jam	jangle
land	lamb	Lang
ran	Rambo	rang
channel	champion	Chang
tan	tambourine	tank
mannequin	mammogram	mango
piano	ammo	anxiety
sandy	Sam	sank

Scrambler: find [ɛ̃ən] as in *can,* [ɛ̃əm] as in *ham* and [ɛ̃ɪŋ] as in *hang.*

1. Frankly, you can't dance, Dan.
2. It began randomly in January.

3. Is he a fantasy man or a family man?
4. Don't dangle my ankle from that angle.
5. Ann's plan is fantastic. Thanks for a fantastic plan, Ann!
6. We can, can't we, Nancy?
7. Sam plays a vampire on that random channel.
8. Frankly, mangos make me anxious.
9. The man went on an angry rampage at the bank.
10. Thanksgiving is all about family and yams.
11. Do you tango or just hang out in the van?
12. Give me a hand with the scrambled mango meringue.
13. And then Rambo's like "bam!" and he ran.
14. I think we can, but I don't know the plan.
15. Amanda can't answer.

> *How do I say ...*
> January?
> [ˈd͡ʒẽənjuˌɛɚi]
> JAN-yoo-air-y

Scrambler: put it all together with [æ], [ẽən], [ẽəm] and [ẽɪŋ].

1. I packed my bags for Africa.
2. On Thanksgiving, I like having yams and cranberry jam with my family.
3. Jack has asthma and can't dance.
4. The actress thanked her fabulous fans.
5. Even January in California is placid.
6. Andrew is an angry adolescent.
7. Actually, the facts add up.
8. Dad asked anxiously about the vaccine.
9. Anne is passionately romantic, but afterwards, sad.
10. Mangoes or apples for the banquet?
11. That's frankly a dramatic tragedy.
12. Dan's bank balance is lacking in cash.

[ɑ:] as in *Thought, Lot,* and *Palm*

A **lexical set** is a group of words that share similar sound features. The words belonging to that set tend to be pronounced the same way in a given dialect. Think of the vowels in *fleece, sea,* and *quiche*. They're spelled differently, but I bet you assign them the same sound in your dialect. Or *daughter, draw,* and *all,* to give a more striking example.[1]

In this section, I suggest that you merge three lexical sets into one pronunciation. Let's try pronouncing *law, lot,* and *lava* with the same vowel. This is somewhat controversial, as many Americans don't do this merger, and some speech teachers may take issue with (and should feel free to adapt) my approach. However, I've found that specifically when training Brits and Aussies, it's helpful to think of the same target sound for all three sets.

Structure

Tongue: touches the lower front teeth and cups downward in the back.
Lips: relaxed (lip corners *may* be *ever so slightly* forward for Set #1).
Jaw: gently lowered.

Set #1 Words

1. awe   paw   law   lawless   claw   saw   draw   raw   jaw   yawn   awning   dawn   lawn   flawed   awkward   awesome   pawing   clawing   sawing   drawing
2. laundry   audience   applause   fraud   August   Santa   Claus   Paul   pause/paws   daughter   taught   caught   naughty   slaughter   launch   authorized   sauce   sausage   faucet   exhaustion   autumn   author   caution   auction   assault
3. ought   bought   fought   thought   brought   broad   broadcast
4. all   hall   appalling   ball   tall   stall   call   small   mall   fall   falling   walls   water   salt   waltz   Walter   false   talk   walk   stalker   chalk
5. (note: these are very short in length)   audition   already   authentic   Caucasian   Australia

Vowels and Diphthongs **13**

Set #1 Phrases

1. yawning at dawn
2. audience applause
3. raw coleslaw
4. fall in the hall
5. salt water
6. unauthorized author
7. thoughtful daughter
8. sausage in sauce
9. chalk drawing
10. stalker's assault
11. walking and talking
12. already autumn

Set #1 Sentences

1. I yawn at small talk.
2. Are you waltzing or walking, Paul?
3. Do you always call it autumn, or fall?
4. Dawn paused in the hall, exhausted, then walked.
5. They saw Santa Claus at the mall.
6. It's already August in Australia.
7. We bought the ball and brought it to Walter.
8. They put salt in the coleslaw, I thought.
9. She called her mother-in-law with caution.

Set #2 Words

1. hop   pop   popular   opposite   top   stop   mop   cop   floppy   shop   tropical   Bob   robbed   sob   Robert   probably   job   hot   not/knot   forgotten   lot   plot   rotten   odd   God   model   modern   rod   occupy   tock   doctor   rock   lock   sock   log   smog   groggy   fog   soggy frog   bomb   comedy   mom   comment   vomit   on   honest   honor   honorable   bond   constant   fond   John   beyond   tongs   donkey   King   Kong   long   prolong   longer   song   strong   doll   dolphin   golf   volume   involve   resolve   solve   dissolve   holiday   dollar college   follow   jolly   cough   off   office   officer   toffee   coffee   loft   soft profit   poverty   cloth   bother   possible   tossing   lost   floss   gloss   across   cross   positive   Roger
2. yacht   watch   swamp   wander   want   wand   wallet   wasp   wash   Washington   squash
3. (note: these words might use [oʊ] in British English, but use [ɑː] in GenAm)   process   progress

14 Vowels and Diphthongs

Set #2 Phrases

1. forgotten the song
2. top dog
3. stop the cops
4. got the job
5. longest song
6. honest to God
7. a holly jolly holiday
8. modern watch
9. wander off
10. soft cloth
11. dollar shop
12. not possible

Set #2 Sentences

1. Was John as popular at college as Rob?
2. The boss at my job gives me holidays off.
3. Washington can be soggy and smoggy when it's hot.
4. The cops stopped the robber across from the shop.
5. Bob lost at golf and resolved to stop bothering.
6. Tom Jolly got involved in office politics.
7. Jon was fond of strong, hot coffee.

Set #3 Words

1. ah   avocado   spa   blah   bra   enchilada   cha   cha   samba   drama   lasagna   iguana   bravo   lava   father   plaza   garage   massage   saga   salsa   nachos   tapas   saké   tacos   Natasha   macho   sonata   karate   kashi   Bach   casa
2. palms   alms   calm   calming   almond   qualms
3. (note: these words might use [æ] in British English, but use [ɑː] in GenAm)   mantra   Nazi   pasta   plaza   Picasso

Set #3 Phrases

1. massage at the spa
2. father's garage
3. bravo for the drama
4. nachos and tacos
5. Bach's sonatas
6. tapas with saké
7. pasta or lasagna?
8. calm the debutante
9. tacos or enchiladas?

Set #3 Sentences

1. Father had qualms, but stayed calm.
2. Are Bach's sonatas from the Renaissance?
3. I prefer cha cha to the samba or the salsa.

4. Do you like salsa with the enchilada or the taco?
5. Ah! Almonds and avocados are calming.
6. Muhammad Ali was macho.
7. "Blah, blah, blah," she said. "I'm so blasé."

> **How do I say ...**
> Renaissance?
> [ˈɹɛnəˌsɑns]
> REN-uh-sans
> Renaissance.

Scrambler: make these vowels identical, or close to it.

1	2	3
awe	opt	ah!
awning	honest	Ana
fault	fond	father
bought	robot	Bali
saw	song	saga
law	lot	la la la
lawn	long	Lana
pawn	pond	papa
talk	tock	taco
bawl/ball	box	balm
call	collie	calm
awful	coffee	cava
naughty	not	Nazi
caught	cotton	Picasso
stalk	stock	Stalin
spawn	respond	spa
pause/paws	possible	pasta
gauze	got	Gaza
draw	drop	drama
awed	odd	avocado

Scrambler:

1. Honestly, father, he's not that tall.
2. John stayed calm amidst the drama.
3. This coffee's awful; it's too hot.
4. He caught the ball but dropped it after all.
5. Cava and pasta are an awesome combo.

6. Tom called my dog from the garage.
7. Father taught us to always be calm.
8. Who saw my wallet? I lost it.
9. He got caught with a lot of tacos.
10. Is it possible to pause the sonata?

[iː] as in *Fleece*

The next two sounds, [iː] as in *fleece* and [uː] as in *goose*, present similar challenges. For most Aussies and many Brits, the tendency will be to do a slight **on-glide**, adding a little "uh" [ə] sound before the vowel itself. Aim to make these **pure vowels**, without an on-glide.

Structure

Tongue: touches the lower front teeth and arches high in the front.
Lips: corners retracted (slight smile).
Jaw: high (back teeth close together).

Words

1. agree bleed deem eel esteem fee feed feel free glee greedy green guarantee heed knee preen queen seed seen sheen succeed three tree creep deep discreet keep geese peep seep sheep sheet speech steep
2. appeal beagle bean breathe congeal cream dean demeanor dream eager eagle ease easy heave leader lean leave meal mean ordeal reveal scream seal squeal tease weave bleach cheat crease each east Easter eat feast feature freak heat increase neat peach preach reap seat speak teach reach
3. bee/Bea flee/flea heel/heal pee/pea peel/peal reed/read reel/real see/sea seem/seam steel/steal tee/tea teem/team
4. Angelina Fiji machine prestige ski chic Costa Rica liter Matisse motif police quiche petite physique Martinique antique unique
5. believe grieve liege Marie seize shield wield receive caffeine ceiling
6. Eve impede concede recede obscene convene scene theme extreme
7. Abby baby belly Betty chewy choosy cooly daddy funny happy heavy honey mommy only pretty puppy

silly thirty wooly baggie biggie calorie camaraderie
Charlie Christie cookie cootie cutie

Phrases

1. a greedy queen
2. Christine's self-esteem
3. Ouija guarantee
4. see the sea
5. illegal bees
6. eat the peach
7. geese from Greece
8. Costa Rican sheep
9. a deep speech
10. Easter feast
11. seized by grief
12. leave the beast
13. agree to succeed
14. Sheila's happy babies
15. yuppie zombies

Sentences

1. Charlie's dream was creepy and extreme.
2. We agreed to three, Abby, see?
3. A vegan feast is even greener, Gene.
4. I've seen Greece, Costa Rica, and Fiji.
5. He's a cutie, but not very unique.
6. The scene was believable, at least.
7. The sea is serene, but freezing.
8. Many calories in these cookies?
9. The police believe my beagle's illegal.
10. Breathe deeply to feel regal.
11. I appreciate the priest's beliefs.
12. Don't scream, Marie, it's only me!

[u:] as in *Goose*

Structure

Tongue: touches the lower front teeth and arches high in the back toward the soft palate.
Lips: corners protrude forward.
Jaw: relaxed.

Words

1. boo   shampoo   goo   moo   too/two   zoo   poodle   noodles   food   boom   doom   loom   zoom   room   balloon   cartoon   spoon   moon   soon   pool   tool   school   cool   foolish   groove   smooth   choose/chews   oops   hoop   boot   root   shoot   proof   tooth   loose   goose   aloof   rooster
2. include   conclude   rude   intrude   crude   Judy   frugal   rumor   June   rule   brute   brutal   Jupiter   truth   sushi   truce   crucial   intrusive   stupid   recruit   fruit   fruitcake   juice   continuity   suit   lawsuit   nuisance   suitcase   swimsuit
3. soup   group   couscous   youth   toucan   coupon   rendezvous   wound
4. prove   approve   move   who   whose/who's   lose
5. grew   threw/through   screw   chew   Jew
6. true   clue   blue/blew   canoe   shoe   bruise   cruise
7. (note: very short) tuition   duplicity   nutrition   superb   boutique   routine   throughout

Phrases

1. juicy sushi
2. cool pool
3. moody blues
4. throughout New York
5. include the conclusion
6. snooty boots
7. school rules
8. couscous and soup
9. truth and rumor
10. remove your swimsuit
11. foolish nuisance
12. true blue

20 Vowels and Diphthongs

Liquid U [ju]

1. you/ewe use usual usually unit
   uniform universe unified unicorn
   debut imbue puny puberty abuse
   future futile mutual cute Cupid
2. mew immune music musical
   amuse
3. cue/queue cube peculiar accuse fusion fuel confusing
   few view review
4. huge hue human
5. youth pupil putrid computer beauty beautiful

> *How do I say ...*
> futile?
> [ˈfjutl̩]
> FYOO-(d)ul
> futile.

Phrases

1. confusing review
2. abusive beauty
3. useful computer
4. universal humanity
5. she argued her view
6. futile youth

Special Topic: to Liquify or Not to Liquify?

When the vowel [u], spelled /u/ or /ew/, follows the consonant sounds [t], [d], [n], and [l] and sometimes [s] and [z], British and Aussie speakers might employ **liquid u** [ju] ("yoo"), or sometimes [tʃu] or [dʒu] ("choo" or "joo"). GenAm speakers hardly ever do. Practice these words using a non-liquid u.

1. Tuesday tune attitude tuna opportunity tulip gratitude
   student tutor tube tuba
2. due duke reproduce introduce duplicate duplex residue
3. new news newspaper renew nuclear nude avenue
4. absolutely salute sleuth Lewis Luke lewd lunar suit
   suitable

Phrases

1. stupid student
2. a new newspaper
3. absolutely less
4. Tuesday's tulips
5. nude duke
6. new attitude
7. avenue duplex
8. overdue opportunity
9. flute tutor

Scrambler: find [u] and [ju]

1. This fruit is too bruised to use.
2. The students got used to the new school's rules.
3. I ordered the blue shoes through Yahoo!
4. Flute music is beautifully soothing.
5. Yoo-hoo! Who's snoozing on duty?
6. He knew all the news before you.
7. The school's computer room is useful and cool.
8. It's usually not prudent to intrude.
9. Do you prefer noodles or couscous with your stew?
10. It's a beautiful Park Avenue duplex.

[ʌ] as in *Strut*

This sound primarily affects northern-English and Irish speakers. Careful not to go to the vowel sound [ʊ] as in *book*.

Structure

Tongue: relaxed down and slightly flattened in the middle.
Lips: relaxed.
Jaw: gently lowered.

Words

1. up puppy cup pub tub rub cut puddle stud duck luck suck instruct ugly hug bug tug rug drug humble summer rum jump under hunter thunder fun hung lung sung rung hungry jungle uncle skunk flunk trunk junk dull seagull ultimate pulse impulse adult cult culture gulp result vulnerable truffle bus discuss muscle lust trust justice fuzz hush blush crush much such judge dumb thumb numb crumb plumbing succumb
2. trouble double touch Doug/dug young tough enough rough cousin blood flood stomach come income ton done Monday month money won/one wonder London tongue among oven hover above dove cover discover government love glove shoves nothing other another mother brother smother southern some/sum son/sun none/nun does doesn't

Phrases

1. double trouble
2. Loving uncle
3. under or above
4. summer fun
5. unjust government
6. something for nothing
7. vulnerable judge
8. rough and tough
9. much money
10. punch it up
11. fuzzy pug
12. young enough
13. hungry seagulls
14. discover another one
15. I won one once

Sentences

1. Seagulls hovered above the doves.
2. The cups are above the oven, honey.
3. Does mother love my uncle, her brother?
4. With luck, I won't stub my thumb.
5. I'm done the first Monday of the month.
6. He indulges in fudge-covered truffles.
7. He's bulked up enough muscle.
8. One doesn't discuss lust on the bus.
9. I was struck dumb by the guns.
10. Too much money for anyone.

Comparison: [ʊ] vs. [ʌ]

The vowel sound [ʊ] is made by slightly arching the back of the tongue toward the soft palate and bringing the lip corners forward. This sound is used in GenAm in words like *book*. Compare it with the flat, unrounded [ʌ] sound, as in *buck*.

[ʊ]	[ʌ]
book	buck
took	tuck
stood	stud
should	shudder
foot	fun
could	cuddle
hood	huddle
full	vulture
pull	pulse
look	luck
bush	blush
wuss	was
would/wood	what

Vowels and Diphthongs

Scrambler: [ʊ] and [ʌ]

1. I understood the cook could cuddle.
2. The lumberjack looked lucky in the woods.
3. This book costs a hundred bucks?
4. I would, and I could, but I wonder if I should.
5. Was football as fun as it once was?

> *How do I say ...*
> what was?
> wʌt, wʌz
> wutt wuzz
> what was.

[oŭ] as in *Goat*

Our first diphthong! Compared to a **pure vowel**, in which your articulators find a position and stay put, a **diphthong** involves combining two vowel sounds into a single syllable. Your articulators move smoothly and swiftly from one position to another.

For [oŭ], most Americans also add a slight on-glide. They start with the near-open central vowel [ɐ] and then go into the diphthong. Have a listen to the audio and try it for yourself.

Structure

Tongue: tip touches lower front teeth, middle cups down, then the back of the tongue arches up as you move through the diphthong.
Lips: corners start neutral, then move forward as you go.
Jaw: gently lowered.

Words

1. flow   blow   glow   slow   mow   tow   row   low   throw   snow   below   know   no   show   bowl   owe   don't   won't   revolting   hope   dope   pope   scope   nope   rope   sober   global   mobile   soda   poke   spoke   coke   focus   joke   broke   moment   diploma   donor   pony   lonely   tofu   both   grocery   dose   post   ocean   noses   motion   emotion   notion   lotion   social   closure
2. alone   clone   phone   robe   globe   explode   code   drove   grove   wove   froze   compose   suppose   expose   hose   chose
3. load   road/rowed   toad/towed   groan/grown   Joan   loaves   loathed   oaths   toad   soap   oat   boat   oak   cloak   soak   loaf   oath   toast   coast   boast   roach   roast   goat
4. woe   Joe   doe   hoe   pro
5. sew/so   owing   growing   blowing   flowing   glowing   slower   lower   slowest

Phrases

1. suppose so
2. home alone
3. oh no!
4. drove the road
5. Roman oath
6. slower growth
7. hoped to elope
8. coast to coast
9. emotional soldier
10. don't boast
11. boatload of oats
12. croaking toad
13. don't go, Joe
14. broke and alone
15. mobile phone

Sentences

1. Do you have roaming on that mobile phone?
2. I won't go home alone! No, no!
3. Roll the dough, then toast the loaves.
4. The joke was told coast to coast and all over the globe.
5. As we drove the roads in the cold, the snow froze.
6. She dozed and rolled over for a moment.
7. Focus, and don't go for all that hocus-pocus!
8. The ocean glowed and flowed below the boat.
9. Does the pope hold a diploma? I don't know.

Special Topic: [oŏɫ] as in *Old*

This can be a tricky combination for some speakers. Go for a dark [ɫ] (see Chapter 2) by lowering the soft palate and lifting the back of the tongue slightly toward it. Keep the lips relaxed and unrounded.

Words

1. poll/pole roll/role toll told old cold sold gold bold hold mold troll hole/whole holy holding coldly soldier folder older molding polling rolling soul/sole fold patrol casserole solar polo solo control polar

Phrases

1. old soul
2. holy scroll
3. soldier's folder
4. cold and moldy
5. a bold troll
6. a solo role
7. holy moly
8. hold the pole
9. solar control

[eɪ] as in *Face*

Structure

Tongue: tip touches the lower front teeth and tongue arches in the front, higher as you move through the diphthong (you may have to think [i] or "ee" as your final sound).
Lips: retracted corners (slight smile).
Jaw: high.

Words

1. pay   day   say   gay   ray   lay   slay   may   stay   bay   Jay   gray   play   tray   clay   way   away   okay   freeway   sideways   subway   saying   praying   staying   paying   graying   crayon
2. stable   table   able   maybe   tomato   potato   grateful   fading   famous   civilization   nation   facial   invasion   navy   gravy   waving   naming   great   break
3. game   same   blame   fame   frame   name   shame   tame   Jane   cane   fade   parade   invade   lemonade   blade   shade   brave   cave   save   craze   laze   age   wage   stage   page   rage   ape   cape   shape   tape   escape   paper   fate   rate   late   mate   state   make   ache   take   rake   lake   snake   naked   fake   shake   taste   space   face   race   grace   brace
4. weigh/way   feign   beige   weight/wait   eight/ate   neighbor   freight
5. aid   paid   raid   laid   frail   snail   rail   trail   quail   afraid   aim   claim   drain   plain   pain   remain   domain   failure   raiding   sailor   dainty   brainy   faith
6. sail/sale   tail/tale   ail/ale   maid/made   praise/prays
7. blasé   matinée   ballet

Phrases

1. pave the way
2. afraid of freeways
3. fade to gray
4. save the day
5. homemade lemonade
6. great debate
7. take up space
8. fading civilization
9. daylight savings
10. graceful and dainty
11. gray, rainy day
12. famous name
13. vague daydream
14. hate mail
15. pray to saints

Sentences

1. Jane was ashamed of her plain name.
2. There's a sale on grapes at Safeway.
3. Is Jason crazy? Or maybe just lazy?
4. Delays on the subway make me insane.
5. Okay, I'll say it: I'm afraid of parades.
6. The famous baseball player got hate mail on a daily basis.
7. My neighbors keep taking my newspaper.
8. Our date was at eight, you're late, and I hate to wait.
9. Did you say "hey" to Jay today?

Mike's "Yogurt Secret"
Many find it tricky to make the tongue arch high enough for the [eī] diphthong. One Brit I coached, Mike, had a revelation that may help you: "Pop a 'y' in it," he said. "Imagine you're about to say 'yogurt.'"
heyyy … *(yogurt)* … hey
Jaaaa … *(yogurt)* … Jane
baaa … *(yogurt)* … baseball
This trick has proven helpful to many other Brits. First, try the words *saying* "yogurt." Then, read the word list just thinking *(yogurt)*

(And by the way) How do I say …
yogurt?
[ˈjoʊgɚt]
YOH-gurt
yogurt.

[aɪ] as in *Price*

Structure

Tongue: tip touches the lower front teeth, and tongue cups down in front. It arches high in the front as you move through the diphthong (again, you may have to think [i:] or "ee" as your final sound).
Lips: retracted corners.
Jaw: gently lowered.

Words

1. high/hi sigh thigh try cry pry dry deny eye July fly shy why sky buy/bye/by guy pie tie die/dye lie skies flies tires cries pies hide side/sighed bride I've drive five lives (n) dive wives lime dime mime crime prime nine spine line bind mind guide acquire inquire require disguise
2. type Skype hype hyper typewriter cycle dynamite spying lying hike like pike tiny shiny vinyl ripe stripe wipe knife life wife white ice lice nice rice advice lilac final climate revival quiet light bright tight alright night fight eyesight frighten right uptight quite

Phrases

1. high time we try
2. July skies
3. dry my eyes
4. sign the line
5. kind of tired
6. hyper tyke
7. right to life
8. bright idea
9. wipe the knife
10. precise advice
11. required vitamins
12. mighty fine life
13. diamond mines
14. white wine
15. high wire

Sentences

1. Cats might have nine lives, but I find mine try to survive.
2. I've decided on white wine with the fried rice tonight.
3. Why fight time? I'm high on life.
4. Keep quiet in the library, or I'll be fined.
5. We're dining at nine, I'd like you to be on time.
6. He gives nice advice, but I think he's lying.
7. His wife was quiet, then sighed.
8. I'm inspired by your lively vitality.
9. There's no privacy in this dry, grimy, pigsty.
10. I fight mime crime in my spare time.

> **Tip:** try Mike's "Yogurt Secret" with [aɪ] as well.
>
> hiiiigh ... (*yogurt*) ... high
> riiigh ... (*yogurt*) ... right

[aʊ] as in *Mouth*

Structure

Tongue: tip touches the lower front teeth, and tongue cups down in the front. As you move through, the back of the tongue arches.
Lips: first retract the lip corners, then push them forward.
Jaw: gently lowered.

Words

1. how   now   cow   allow   vow   wow   eyebrow   frown   down   brown   drown   crown   owl   howl   prowl   fowl/foul   sound   hound   rebound   pound   round   ground   cloud   loud   proud   noun   mouth   house   arouse   lounge
2. powder   flower/flour   tower   drowning   growling   powerful   ounce   bounce   count   accountant   announce   out   trout   about   stout   doubt   drought   cloudy   mouse   loudly   proudly   thousand   arousing   our/hour   sour   couch   slouch   south

Phrases

1. proud of our hounds
2. brown owls
3. loud and proud
4. around town
5. powerful doubts
6. out of the house
7. about an hour
8. slouchy blouse
9. loud shouting
10. crouched down
11. frowning eyebrows
12. flower-covered gown

Sentences

1. My hound growled proudly at the sound.
2. It took us an hour to get downtown.
3. Wow! The clouds are out down south!
4. I found out about your foul mouth.
5. The trout swam toward the sound.
6. I doubt pouting is allowed.

7. Too crowded now. How about we go out?
8. She's grouchy around the house.
9. Ouch! Get out the towel, now!
10. Crouch down and sneak around town.

Note

1 I am indebted to the work of J.C. Wells and his description of lexical sets.

2
T AND L

Introduction to T

The unsung hero of GenAm consonants! GenAm has (by my count) six pronunciations of [t], and precise treatment of them can make all the difference. The ones we will cover are **voiced**, **held**, **glottalized**, and **vanishing**. The others—**aspirated** (as in *time*) and **dentalized** (as in *get there*)—you probably already do in your native dialect.

Voiced [t]

Voiced [t̬] (which you can think of as an almost-[d]) occurs between vowels, when [t] starts an unstressed syllable. In other words, you'd use it in *Italy*, but not *Italian*.

Words

1. atom   Italy   attic   butter   better   letter   water   heater   Betty   sweater
2. meeting   pity   footing   autograph   Saturday   computer   cavity   feta

Phrases

Note that voiced [t̬] also appears between words to create a smooth flow. Use it when a [t] ends a word and you want to link into a vowel right away ("ride-away").

1. not a
2. not again
3. leave it alone
4. set it
5. fought a
6. forget about it
7. write a letter
8. let her (drop h)
9. get him (drop h)
10. right away
11. get all
12. get it around
13. we meet again
14. get it a better sweater
15. caught another

Sentences

1. Set it on the little metal table.
2. Not another cavity! I got a cavity.
3. Get a better sweater, Betty.
4. Can you write it in a letter?
5. Put it in a little water bottle.
6. Get all the turtles in the metal gutter.
7. I bought a bit of fatter feta for the frittata.
8. It's a pity the meeting didn't go better.
9. Get all the data in the computer and boot it up.

Special Topic: *To*

Another interesting use of voiced [t̬] occurs in the word *to*, in certain positions. You can voice the [t] in *to* when it follows a vowel (as in "go to bed") or a voiced consonant (as in "mean to go").

A **voiced consonant** is any consonant that vibrates when you articulate it, such as [b], [d], [g], [m], [n], [ŋ], [v], [z] and [l]. If you're unsure whether a consonant is voiced, put your hand on your throat as you say it. If you feel vibration, it probably is. Practice these phrases using a voiced [t̬] to ensure a smooth connection.

Phrases

1. when to do it
2. free to try
3. sad to see you go
4. beg to differ
5. hang to dry
6. same to me
7. ran to my side
8. mean to be there
9. children together
10. further to go
11. eager to see it
12. happier to do it
13. tell her to go
14. married to me
15. call her to tell her
16. see her to the door
17. cater to him
18. leader to beat
19. harder to get there
20. go to lunch
21. mine to say
22. hand to hand combat
23. another to deal with
24. mother to my child
25. father to my daughter
26. trying to get there
27. person to commit a crime
28. crazier to judge
29. faster to process
30. learn to play
31. order to follow
32. over to me
33. sorry to hear that
34. love to do it
35. loved to do it
36. shoulder to cry on
37. man to man
38. over to my uncle
39. live to eat
40. honor to be nominated
41. we plan to go out
42. told you to do it
43. pleasure to serve you
44. better to know
45. sadder to see
46. letter to Laura more to do
47. little to myself
48. for here or to go
49. need to know
50. color to paint with
51. call her to apologize
52. remember to do
53. eager to please
54. dream to remember
55. remember to ask her to try
56. four to six
57. daughter to me
58. when to do it
59. go to work
60. quarter to three
61. only way to get it
62. closer to the teeth

Glottalized T [ʔ]

The glottis is the space between your vocal folds. Sometimes before a vowel, you might close the glottis to add clarity or emphasis (as in "uh oh!"). If you come from London or Scotland, chances are you already use glottal stops in your speech.

In GenAm, [t] may be replaced by a glottal stop—the phonetic symbol is [ʔ]—before [k] as in *camp*, [g] as in *goal*, [b] as in *boy*, [ɹ] as in *red*, [w] as in *wait* and [m] as in *move*. Leave the tip of the tongue down.[1]

[ʔk] Phrases

1. sitcom
2. it can
3. might calm
4. it can't compare
5. not careful
6. fat cat
7. but casually
8. great car
9. quite quiet

[ʔg] Phrases

1. not good
2. it got going
3. at Gordon's
4. went great
5. I can't go
6. is it gonna work?
7. not green
8. fit guy
9. won't grow

[ʔb] Phrases

1. not bad
2. got bigger
3. fat bonus
4. can't begin
5. a lot better
6. don't bargain
7. but basically
8. sit back
9. is it burning?

[ʔɹ] Phrases

1. that really
2. not really
3. not right
4. not ready
5. get ready
6. is it real?
7. not ridiculous
8. can't really
9. at Rachel's

[ʔw] Phrases

1. that way
2. it wasn't
3. it was
4. what was
5. can't wait
6. it would
7. that one
8. not why
9. right way
10. that wish
11. but why
12. get one
13. not what
14. went well
15. bright white

[ʔm] Phrases

1. hit me
2. got may
3. not Mike
4. fat man
5. get mad
6. hot mic
7. bit my tongue
8. white mouse
9. want more

Sentences

1. But why should it be that way?
2. A sitcom might calm her down.
3. It's not ready, it's not right.
4. I want that one, I can't wait.
5. It went well after it got going.
6. Quit complaining and get ready.
7. That root canal really can't wait.
8. Look at that bright white cat.
9. It was quite quiet, Kerry.
10. I'm at Rachel's, not at Gordon's.

Held [t̚]

To make held [t̚], lift the tip of the tongue to the gum ridge, as if you are going to say *tee*. But instead of releasing the tip with a puff of air, hold it in place. The effect is a sense of the [t], but without the release. Almost like you're eating it or keeping it secret.

Held [t̚] occurs before a consonant sound in the same word, the next word, or—*this is crucially different from British English*—before a pause.

Phrases

1. What?
2. not feeling it
3. didn't know
4. get down
5. Stop it!
6. I bet.
7. Don't be late.
8. Aunt Sally
9. I can't.
10. You don't?
11. I won't.
12. quite silly
13. get it out
14. can't find it
15. haters gonna hate
16. figured out
17. can't do it
18. fix it
19. outnumbered
20. fitness
21. pitstop
22. quit dancing
23. fit for it
24. thought so
25. notebook
26. butler
27. Great Neck
28. sit down
29. heatstroke
30. get drunk

The exceptions are [ptʰ] as in *apt*, [ktʰ] as in *fact*, [ftʰ] as in *lift* and [stʰ] as in *fast*—these [t] sounds are aspirated, with a little puff of air (indicated by the [ʰ] symbol phonetically).

1. apt   napped   heaped   stopped   ripped   rapt   capped
2. pact   fact   react   attract   tract   picked   wrecked   instruct
3. craft   laughed   miffed   sift   wolfed   loft   soft
4. fast   just   rust   must   cast   last   roast   toast   mast   passed

Scrambler: find held [t̚], glottalized [ʔ] and voiced [t̬]

1. Betty's got it all figured out.
2. I bet he's got it all figured out.
3. I can't get down, I can't get out.
4. He can't let go of it.
5. Is he into football in Great Neck?
6. They got drunk and quit trying.
7. How's his fitness? Is he fit for it?
8. Stop it! I hate it! Will you quit it?
9. My notebook is not so notable, so forget it.
10. Can't get in on the act?

> *How do I say...*
> figure?
> [ˈfɪgjɚ]
> FIG-yer
> figure.

Vanishing [t]

It's quite common for [t] to disappear altogether when it follows [n] and goes into an unstressed vowel sound, either in the same word (*internet* becomes "innernet") or the next word (*I sent a card* becomes "I senna card").

Probably more than the other versions of [t], this one is best treated with some inconsistency. Many speakers, myself included, will sometimes use an aspirated [tʰ] instead. It depends on how quickly we're speaking and how much emotional impact we want to give to the word. Try it and see what feels right for you in the moment.

Phrases

1. internet
2. dentist
3. printer
4. enter
5. went into
6. sent a card
7. entertainment
8. interface
9. intercontinental
10. pint of berries
11. plant a tree
12. can't I do one
13. interstate
14. interfere
15. interactive
16. international
17. twenty
18. pentagon
19. Santa Claus
20. Antarctica
21. won't even go
22. hasn't he
23. isn't he
24. aren't I
25. won't he
26. doesn't he
27. didn't it
28. Toronto
29. interview

Sentences

1. He won't even try to go.
2. My dentist isn't even on the internet.
3. My interview for the job in Toronto is tomorrow.
4. Doesn't he get a chance to enter?
5. Didn't her mom plant a tree in the intercontinental garden?
6. Santa Claus is certainly entertaining.
7. This printer has terrible interface, doesn't it?
8. He went into shock when he realized he couldn't even do it.

Introduction to L

This shift primarily affects Aussies but may interest some Brits depending on your dialect of origin.

Broadly speaking, GenAm uses two L sounds, **light [l]** and **dark [ɫ]**. Light [l] is used in *prevocalic* (pre-vowel) positions, such as *light* and *alive*. It launches a syllable. To make it, touch the tip of the tongue *and the very front of the blade* to the gum ridge. The voice passes over the lowered sides of the tongue as you move quickly into the following vowel.

Dark [ɫ] occurs in *postvocalic* (post-vowel) positions. Think *ill*, *feel*, *dull*, *cold*. For this sound, the soft palate lowers, and the back of the tongue lifts slightly towards it (imagine you're gargling). Aussies tend to have dark [ɫ] in their dialect, but not Light [l].

There is no lip-rounding associated with L in GenAm.

Words for Light [l]

1. lips   lift   let   lack   lurk   luck   love   Lou   look   law   lot   llama   lay   lie   Lloyd   low   loud   Lear   lair   liar   lore
2. blather   flabby   glad   glib   glory   clatter   flip   clothes   close   blood   blue   glamorous   play   slander   slay   black   blow   bland   claw   clamp   flew
3. elongate   Allen   alive   elegant   illegitimate   illegal   foolish   Billy   killer   ability   belly   valley   ruler   bully   filing   pulling   girlish   billion   million   Lily   hello

Words for Dark [ɫ]

1. meal   eel   feel   ill   will   fell   bell   hell   Al   pal   full   bull   pull   Paul   call   tall   doll   film   elm   scalp   help   field   wield   grilled   twelve   himself   dissolve   repulse   eels   cools   silk   people   evil   needle   beetle   special   minimal   animal   eagle   pickle   hostile   noodle   kettle
2. cold   old   pole   goal   soul   role/roll   hole/whole   toll   told   gold
3. earl   girl   hurl   pearl   Carl   snarl

Scrambler: try to identify the light [l] and dark [ɫ] below.

1. I'd love a little liquor, Larry.
2. Is that a metal kettle on the griddle?
3. I'll have twelve heaping helpings of alfalfa.
4. Evil people repulse Ursula.
5. With luck, I won't look like a liar.
6. Lily is philosophical and glamorous, but cold.
7. It would take a million dollars to relocate to Iceland.
8. Can I help you feel your feelings?
9. Are you looking to live in the village?
10. That howling sound was an owl on the prowl.

Note

1 The glottal stop is a very contemporary, casual sound and may not be suitable for all material or performance circumstances. Use it for stories set in the present-day and know that if you're working in a large theater, you may need to modify this.

3
R

Introduction to R

The "R" sound was very tricky for me. Either I wouldn't hit it, or I'd hit it too hard and my throat would become tight and sound strangled.
—Oliver Thornton, from Wales and London

Felt like I had a golf ball in my mouth every time I tried to say something like order, *or my least favorite word:* further.
—Michael Dale, from London

You knew we'd get here eventually. To begin, let's get a sense of the difference between **consonant R** as in *read*, *rip*, *ready* and **vocalic R** as in *here*, *car*, and *stir*.

Consonant R initiates a syllable. Without it, the word would not make sense. Chances are, you already have a mastery of it—you use it all the time. To make it, lift and retract the tip of your tongue. The vibration of your voice passes between the tongue tip and your gum ridge as you launch into a vowel. (Note that if you normally round your lips when you make this sound, you should leave your lips relaxed in GenAm.)

Let's try a few consonant R words. Focus on feeling the sensation of the R you already know. What effort is required to make it?

read   red   royal   route   rosé   rustic   romantic   risky   roundabout   run

Note that consonant R needn't only appear at the beginning of a word. It can be in the middle as in *around*, *arrest*, and *forensic*. The point is that it energizes and gives sense to the following syllable.

So, you've got that. The one that can be tricky is vocalic R which finishes or "rounds off" a vowel sound. It comes at the end of a syllable. To make it, lift and retract the tip of your tongue, and—this is crucial—brace the back sides of your tongue against the upper back molars. That foundation back there will give you an anchor and help you lift the tongue with less tension.

car   there   beer   care   careful   barman   doormat   floor   sharper   clear

Don't worry if you sound funny at first. It's a delicate balance. If you go too far, you feel like a pirate. If you do too little, it doesn't happen. Keep trying, and don't be afraid to be bold at first.

Now let's work on some vocalic R, also referred to as "r-coloring."

[ɝː] as in *Nurse*

Structure

Tongue: lifts up and back with back sides braced against back upper molars.
Lips: neutral.
Jaw: relaxed.

Words

1. sir   stir   firm   squirm   girl   swirl   curl   hurl   virgin   bird   her   were   herb   herbal   nerd   prefer   concern   permanent   term   merge   nervous   deserve   serve   service   iceberg   Germany   early   learn   pearl   earn/urn   chauffeur   monsieur   connoisseur   coiffeur   journey   journal   journalist   purr   occur   blur   urban   curb   murder   absurd   murmur   burn   nocturnal   surgery   urge   urgent   splurge   further   Thursday   curve   furniture   word   world   worm   colonel/kernel
2. dirt   flirt   shirt   skirt   thirty   thirsty   first   circus   circumstance   quirky   chirp   birth   birthday   virtue   herpes   certain   dessert   alert   person   jerk   earth   rehearse   search   courteous   courtesy   burp   slurp   purpose   purple   burst   curse   purse   nurse   turkey   hurt   Kurt/curt   surf   church   nurture   work   workout   worse   worship   worth

Phrases

1. worship at church
2. nurture courtesy
3. thirsty girls
4. flirt in a skirt
5. a worse purse
6. quirky nurse
7. dirty worms
8. absurd service
9. deserve dessert
10. chirping birds
11. the colonel's hurt
12. earth's curves

Sentences

1. The early bird deserves the worm.
2. Is the turkey hurt? Or just perturbed?
3. Does the perky nurse work on Thursdays?
4. He searched the earth for the perfect girl.
5. Bert and Ernie weren't cursing at the church service.
6. Does Surf 'n' Turf serve dessert?
7. The girl purchased a journal for her thirteenth birthday.
8. That purple shirt is perfect for a certain nerdy person.

> **How do I say ...**
> herb?
> [ɝːb]
> URB
> herb.

Special Topic: A New Use of [ɝː]

While it may sound funny at first, try using [ɝː] in the following words and phrases.

Words

1. curious   tourist   courier   plural   assuring   reassuring   insurance   luxurious   Missouri   jury   pure   mature   immature   premature   cure   endure   manicure   pedicure   secure   obscure   security   purely   urine   Europe   purity   purer   bureau   durable   mural   obscurity   furious   fury   sure
2. courage   curry   borough/burrow   currency   Murray   thorough   furrow   nourish   hurricane   worry   hurry   surrogate   flourish   flurry

Phrases

1. furious tourist
2. Europe's bureaus
3. curiously immature
4. security insurance
5. premature manicure
6. currently furious
7. purer urine
8. durable mural
9. secure currency

Sentences

1. It's just a flurry, don't worry Murray.
2. What's the current currency in Europe?
3. I'm worried about the curry in Missouri.
4. A luxurious manicure and pedicure is the cure.
5. I'm sure the jury reached a verdict prematurely.
6. Can you ensure it's durable and secure in a hurricane?
7. It's a courageous and thorough bureau.
8. Can that mural endure in obscurity?
9. Sure, it's her surrogate, sir.

[ɚ] as in *Letter*

This sound is nearly identical to [ɝː], except it only appears in unstressed syllables. That's an added challenge, as you must sneak the R sound in quite quickly.

Structure

Tongue: lifts up and back with back sides braced against back upper molars.
Lips: neutral.
Jaw: relaxed.

Words

1. Bermuda Bernard murder western energy eastern southern liberty government reservation Saturday leopard forbid actor author prior labor neighbor visitor liquor senator favor professor discover lover theater brother mother sister father happier fewer never
2. standard Saturn survive measure wizard vineyard sugary treasure creature supper forget effort stubborn Easter anger finger tiger survivor power paper officer teacher

Phrases

1. Easter weather
2. discovered lover
3. featherbed dreamer
4. treasured reminder
5. vineyard pleasures
6. particular color
7. wonderful feature
8. never on Saturday
9. father's daughter
10. sharper scissors
11. stubborn neighbor
12. Officer Bernard

Sentences

1. My father, my mother, sister, and brothers are visitors.
2. I never wear leather to the theater, except on Saturday.
3. You'll never get thinner having liquor with dinner.
4. The winner never pictured failure.
5. Don't forget to offer the neighbor a favor.

> *How do I say ...*
> Bernard?
> [bɚˈnɑɚd]
> bur-NARD
> Bernard.

[ɪɚ] as in *Near*

Vocalic R can also appear at the end of diphthongs. You'll start with your tongue tip down behind the lower front teeth, then raise and retract it to make r-coloring as you move through the diphthong.

Structure

Tongue: tip starts at lower front teeth, arching high in the front, then lifts up and back as you find r-coloring.
Lips: slightly retracted.
Jaw: high.

Words

1. ear   appear   spear   gear   near   smear   clear   fear   rear   year   neared   weary   ears   clearance   dreary   spearmint   yearbook   fearful   frontier   premier   pierce   fierce   cashier   weird   bier/beer   pier/peer   tier/tear   steer   cheer   career   engineer   Cheerio   volunteer   deer/dear   leer/Lear   mere   we're   adhere   interfere   sincere   sphere   here/hear   serious   delirious   experience   souvenir
2. spirit   mirror   material   pyramid   pirouette   period   virile   satirical   lyrical

Phrases

1. appear clearly
2. dreary year
3. smeared tears
4. weird earrings
5. jeer and sneer
6. "cheers!" over beers
7. mirror here
8. King Lear's fears
9. adhere to experience
10. volunteer cashier
11. engineering career
12. Zaire souvenir
13. sheared his beard
14. rear pier
15. virile deer

Sentences

1. Her pierced ears are fierce.
2. What a weird souvenir from Zaire.
3. "We're here!" they cheered with spirit at the New Year.

4. We're clearly fearful of our careers.
5. She's delirious and can't hear us from here.
6. I'm a volunteer cashier at the clearance sale year after year.
7. Seriously, I'm being sincere, my dear!
8. Is it merely your period? Or is it more severe?
9. They neared delirium every time he appeared.
10. She appeared fearlessly serious at the hearing.

[ɛɚ] as in *Square*

Structure

Tongue: tip touches lower front teeth to start, cupping slightly down, then lifts up and back as find r-coloring.
Lips: slightly retracted.
Jaw: relaxed.

Words

1. care barely compare dare rare scare share glare daredevil square careless barefoot caretaker declare nightmare prepared software parent transparent caring various rarer air despair repair chair affair dairy hair/hare fair/fare pair/pare/pear stair/stare upstairs downstairs airwave airfare airplane unfair millionaire
2. bear/bare wear/ware/where tear (rip) somewhere anywhere nowhere elsewhere where's there/their/they're

Phrases

1. careful there
2. scared of nightmares
3. caring parent
4. somewhere out there
5. unfair comparison
6. software nightmare
7. stare in despair
8. hairy bears
9. they're millionaires
10. wear their hair
11. daring affair
12. repair housewares

Sentences

1. Even caring parents can seem unfair.
2. Mary's scared of airplanes and can't bear to go anywhere.
3. I'm in despair! My software needs repair.
4. Be careful with their chairs, they're rare heirlooms.
5. The daredevil was careless and barely prepared.
6. Airfare to anywhere is a nightmare.

Special Topic: A New Use of [ɛɚ]

While it may sound funny at first, try using [ɛɚ] in the following words and phrases.

Words

1. Mary/marry/merry   arrow   Harry/hairy   narrow
   Arabic   paragraph   Paris   paradox   comparison   parasite
   carry/Carrie/Kerry   Barry   Carol carrot/carat   character
   guarantee   marathon   narrator   narrate   sparrow   clarity
   charity   parish   apparel   Sarah   Larry   barricade   marrow
   apparent
2. America   Eric   error   heritage   perish   terror   terrible   therapy
   merrier   generic   ferry/fairy   cherry   cherish   prosperity
   very   sherry   ceremony   Gerald   terrace   derelict   heroine
   herald   Meredith

Phrases

1. Herald Square
2. American Apparel
3. Harry's posterity
4. terrible therapy
5. perish in terror
6. a very merry character
7. guaranteed heritage
8. generic heroine
9. Barry Fitzgerald
10. cherished fairies
11. a narrow comparison
12. carrots for the sparrow

Sentences

1. Careful, Carol—Harry's very hairy.
2. Sarah narrated with clarity, but Meredith was barely there.
3. Carrie Kerry's heritage is a paradox.
4. I go to American Apparel for generic underwear.
5. Does Eric care for carrots?
6. It's a cherry sherry, Larry.
7. A parasite? In Mary's marrow? What a terror!
8. There was an error, apparently.
9. "Narrate!" said the narrator about the narrative. "It's narration!"
10. You look terrible, Barry. You need therapy. Or Paris.

[ɔɚ] as in *Force*

Structure

Tongue: tip touches lower front teeth to start, arching high in the back, then lifts up and back as you find r-coloring.
Lips: forward.
Jaw: relaxed down.

Words

1. door floor doorman adore shore explore gore
more ignore score store chore snore hoard sore/soar
bore/boar scoreboard sophomore sycamore roar
oar hoarse/horse board aboard floorboard uproar
stork fork pork afford lord ordinary order orchestra
ornate ornament organ organization short sort resort
sorbet fort metaphor extraordinary mortgage storm form
normal inform performance formal hormones torment
torture torn born corn north portion orchard Mormon
court four/for fourth/forth mourning/morning source
course/coarse fluorescent
2. war/wore warn/worn warm swarm warp wart
wharf dwarf drawer

Phrases

1. warm morning
2. mortgage foreclosure
3. extraordinary score
4. affordable store
5. ignore the chores
6. swore in court
7. adore the seashore
8. ornate ornaments
9. portion of corn
10. dormant hormones
11. force the course
12. boring report

Sentences

1. We ordered pork with corn, of course.
2. Store your shorts in the warm-weather drawer.
3. It's an ordinary, affordable store.
4. It's not normal to ignore the score.
5. What's the source of this gory war?
6. I was born in Georgia but grew up in Norway.
7. The orchestra's fourth performance was too formal.
8. I warned you not to bore the doorman with your stories, George.
9. It's an extraordinary organization, Lori.

> **How do I say ...**
> organization?
> [ˌɔɚgənəˈzeɪʃən]
> OR-guh-nuh-ZAY-shin

Special Topic: A New Use of [ɔɚ]

Match the sounds in column 1 and column 2, using [ɔɚ] in both sets of words.

1	2
or	orange, orifice, oracle, Oregon
hoard	horror, horoscope, abhorrence, horrible, Horowitz
tore	torrid, torrent, historical, Dorothy
core	coronation, incorrigible, correspond, coral
more	moral, immoral, Morris
floor	Florida, florist, Florence, Laurel, Laurence
four	forest, foreign, forehead, foray, forage
Thor	authority
war/wore	warrant, warrior
quarter	quarrel, quarantine
nor	seniority, minority, majority
pour	poor, porridge, Boris

Sentences

1. My horoscope was horrible.
2. The core of the story was immoral.
3. The poor orator from Florida had no authority.
4. Historically, Florence was foreign.
5. Which orifice was immoral or most abhorrent?
6. Was there a warrant for the war?
7. Don't quarrel with Thor; he has seniority and authority.
8. The orator had no authority to start a foreign war.
9. Authority comes from the minority of the organization.
10. I was born in Georgia but grew up in Florida.
11. Four-door Fords lack authority.
12. More in the morning, Dorothy.

[ɑɚ] as in *Start*

Structure

Tongue: tip touches lower front teeth to start, cupping down in the back, then lifts up and back as you find r-coloring.
Lips: neutral.
Jaw: relaxed down.

Words

1. car bar far harm jar mar Mark par park part
   star spark bark shark sharp scar cigar pardon guitar
   radar bizarre garbage marble art article start garden
   remarkable argument argue bargain arm harmless alarm
   charming barn darn carnival Charlie scarf carve
   farther harsh Marcia/Marsha Mars march Argentina
   margin charge large harp Arkansas guard lifeguard
   sergeant heart/hart hearth
2. our/are sorry borrow tomorrow sorrow

Phrases

1. large and in charge
2. harsh remark
3. hard-hearted Margaret
4. garbage in the park
5. far from the market
6. Charlie's art
7. guard the garden
8. sharp bark
9. the farm's barn
10. jarring alarm
11. March in Arkansas
12. starving and parched
13. card shark
14. darkest part
15. far, farther, farthest

Sentences

1. It's harder and harder to part with Mark.
2. No parking after dark in the market parking lot.
3. We *are* far from our bar, Charlie.
4. In my heart, I pardon that harsh remark.
5. That scarf is marvelous and artfully bizarre.

6. I have his card, it's charming, but what does he charge?
7. I don't have the heart to argue, Marsha. Sorry.
8. My dog barked sharply at the parked car.
9. Tomorrow I'm going to borrow the car from Lars. It's ours!

R to TH

Aim for a soft, easy transition between vocalic R and TH, guided by the tip of the tongue.

Phrases

1. earthly earth
2. nevertheless
3. paper the ceiling
4. do you hear that?
5. suffer the consequences
6. under the table
7. where the wild things are
8. never the victim
9. tear the sheets
10. over there, though
11. scare the kids
12. better that way
13. up there though
14. wear their hair down
15. aware that they do
16. near the computer
17. hair that is blue
18. under their breath
19. where the heck is it?
20. care that way
21. water the plants
22. wear the coat
23. for the kids
24. other than that
25. farther to go
26. further to go
27. pour the drinks

Sentences

1. Where's the colder-weather clothing?
2. She's never the victim; she weathers the storms of this life.
3. Did you hear the thunder over there?
4. It's better that way, even though it's harder to hear that.
5. Don't scare the kids in the apartment.
6. It's hardly in order for her to herd the horses.
7. Where were they the first Thursday in February?
8. Nevertheless, you'll have to paper the ceiling.
9. I'm aware that they do, but I don't care that they share that.
10. If we tear these sheets, will they absorb the torrential downpour, though?
11. Up there, though? Or maybe over there?

Intrusive R

Avoid adding an R between the vowels in these phrases. Instead, anchor the tongue tip to the back of the lower teeth for the transition. The resulting vowel blend should feel loose (and yes, maybe a bit inebriated). Think "Anna⁀and I" (not "Anna<u>r</u> and I").

Phrases

1. Alma allowed it
2. Anna ached for it
3. China is big
4. China and Japan
5. Asia on the rise
6. Alaska isn't far
7. Alaska and Hawaii
8. Alaska or Russia
9. Santa is fat
10. Santa and Rudolf
11. Santa always makes is
12. sofa and chair
13. the sofa is overstuffed
14. sofa or couch
15. America ended it
16. America always does
17. America is what it is
18. a llama is walking
19. a llama isn't here
20. a llama always is

Sentences

1. Amanda ended her friendship with Jessica in February.
2. Anna Adams put the data in the computer.
3. Will Emma ever get her sofa upholstered?
4. I saw it! I saw a saw in the garage.
5. California is not like Alabama, am I right?
6. Scuba is prohibited in the plaza area, I think.
7. That comma is a flaw in the sentence.
8. I'm in awe of Alaska and Antarctica in the winter.
9. My bra is back at the spa, I'm afraid.
10. It's a saga of impossible drama and suspense.
11. The pasta is always the draw in this restaurant.
12. Canada Airlines offers flights to Asia and Africa.
13. Dracula is in Transylvania, isn't he?
14. In India, vanilla and chocolate are even better.
15. Is he sore after the saw attack?
16. The china is out, so dinner is on its way.
17. The plaza opened on November eleventh.
18. Tessa and Roger ended it.
19. Pour out the sauce, the raw oysters are served!

Fluffy Suffixes

These word endings are more drawn-out in GenAm, with an element of secondary stress on the second-to-last syllable. "MAN-duh-TORY-y." "SOL-uh-TARE-y." It may take some practice to fully expand that second-to-last syllable. Let it feel a little chewy, like you have a wad of gum in your mouth.

Words

1. [ɔɚi] mandatory auditory inflammatory circulatory laboratory conservatory repertory obligatory dormitory oratory explanatory reformatory depository accusatory allegory category celebratory suppository
2. [ɛɚi] dictionary solitary stationary cemetery ordinary binary corollary culinary library disciplinary extraordinary hereditary honorary military necessary arbitrary voluntary ordinary literary planetary cautionary secretary temporary vocabulary February sanitary customary honorary primary January strawberry raspberry blackberry gooseberry
3. [oʊni] matrimony alimony ceremony testimony

Sentences

1. Do you carry a suppository for the inflammatory depository?
2. It's ordinarily a voluntary testimony, never mandatory. But it's arbitrary.
3. Is there a literary library in the laboratory?
4. I like cranberry sauce and gooseberries in January. It must be hereditary.
5. This repertory company is extraordinary.
6. It's customary for secretaries to eat strawberries.
7. Sarah's primary vocabulary is far from ordinary.
8. Allegories are necessary cautionary stories.
9. Is solitary confinement a necessary disciplinary action?
10. At least it's sanitary, and only temporary, so let's not be too accusatory.

4
ELISION

Elision is the fancy word for "make it sound a little drunk." If you've ever been told your GenAm is good, but doesn't sound "natural" enough, this might be the ticket. In this chapter, we'll explore options for blending words together to create a smooth flow. This takes courage and practice. It also takes trust in yourself and your ear.

Note: these are options only, new colors to add to your palette rather than rules. While the proper use of elision will work wonders for your fluency in GenAm, be advised that American speakers use elision inconsistently depending on their age, the speed at which they're speaking, and the stakes of the situation. Not every elision will be right for every scene, so use your judgment.

I'm Going To

This elision only works when speaking in the future tense using another verb, as in "I'm going to call her tomorrow." It doesn't work when speaking about physically going somewhere, as in "I'm going to the park." Also, it only works in the first person singular.

Looks Like	Sounds Like	As In
I'm going to	Imunna	Imunna try.

Sentences

1. I'm going to sing this weekend at the party.
2. I'm going to go on vacation to Iceland.
3. I'm going to say hello to Ella.
4. I'm going to try to dress better.
5. I'm going to learn to do a handstand.
6. I'm going to quit next Tuesday.
7. I'm going to get there eventually.
8. I'm going to have to see about that.
9. I'm going to try to learn more accents.
10. I'm going to learn Swedish in my spare time.
11. I'm going to try to see if I can find him.
12. I'm going to go vegan next year.
13. I'm going to get there if it's the last thing I do.
14. I'm going to go to the farmer's market on Friday.
15. I'm going to fix the car as soon as I get paid.

> **Tip:** Don't ask Americans if they do this elision. They will deny it and say it sounds low-class. Better to just casually ask them about their weekend plans, sit back, and listen to the "Imunnas" pour forth. They will!

Why Don't You/Let Me/Trying To

Looks Like	**Sounds Like**	**As In**
why don't you	whyncha	Whyncha give it a try?
let me	lemmee	Lemme give it a try.
trying to	tryna	I'm tryna to give it a try.

Sentences

1. Why don't you see if you can do it?
2. Let me see if I can find it.
3. I'm trying to get more practice in this weekend.
4. Why don't you want to?
5. Let me give him a call.
6. She's trying to pin us down about the date.
7. Why don't you see if you can get him on the phone.
8. Yeah, but can you let me do it?
9. We're only trying to help.
10. Why don't you try to make a change?
11. Can you just let me have a second, please?
12. What are you trying to do, exactly, George?
13. Why don't you let your guard down a little?
14. Oh! Let me see!
15. Sit down! I'm trying to see.
16. I don't know if she's going to let me do it. ("gunna lemmee")
17. Why don't you let me go with him? ("whyncha lemme")
18. I'm trying to save money this month.
19. Let me text her, and then let me see what she says.
20. Why don't you relax and let me take care of it?
21. I could try if you would let me catch my breath!
22. I'm trying to relax over here!

66 Elision

Is This/Is That/Is There and Was This/Was That/Was There

Looks Like	**Sounds Like**	**As In**
is this/was this	izzis/wuzzis	Izzis yours? Wuzzis yours?
is that/was that	izzat/wuzzat	What izzat? What wuzzat?
is there/was there	izzere/wuzzere	Where izzere a cab? Wuzzere a fight?

Sentences

1. Is this your car?
2. Is that a dog or a cat?
3. Is there a problem here?
4. Was this your grandmother's?
5. What was that he was saying?
6. Was there a delay on the subway?
7. Is this one of those new ones?
8. Where was this one taken?

Dialogue

Try out the dialogue below. Fill in the blanks with your own answers

A: Is this the photo album from your vacation?
B: Oh, is there some interest in looking through it?
A: Is that what I implied?
B: I was there last year.
A: Where was this?
B: My hometown. You know, _____.
A: Is that a town or a city?
B: Little of both.
A: Where was that one taken?
B: Is that ... right, that was at my first school, _____.

A: Who is that next to you in the picture?
B: He was this guy I roped into posing with me. *(pause)* What?
A: Nothing. Was there … *(pause)*
B: What, is that a problem? Is that a smirk on your face?
A: Is that what you want to see?

68 Elision

It's/That's

Make this elision very subtle and use it only at the beginning of a sentence.

Looks Like	Sounds Like	As In
it's	ts	ts a big deal
that's	ats	ats not what I heard.

Sentences

1. It's not a big deal. What? It's not!
2. It's only temporary.
3. That's not really the point.
4. It's not like it's forever.
5. It's quite an accomplishment.
6. That's a great idea.
7. It's good to get a new perspective.

Dialogue

A: It's good, isn't it?
B: It's not bad, yeah.
A: It's *good*.
B: That's what I meant.
A: It's great. I mean. Come on. It's *great*.
B: That's—yeah. It's great. *(pause)*
A: That's so like you.
B: It's—what's so like me?
A: "It's not bad." Psh.
B: It's *amazing*, okay? It's just …
A: It's what?
B: It's just not my taste.
A: That's hard to believe.
B: It's the truth.
A: That's too bad.
B: It's not, actually.

Should We? Could We? Can We?

Looks Like	Sounds Like	As In
should we	shwee	Shwee try it?
could we	kwee	Kwee get there?
can we	knwe	When knwe talk?

Sentences

1. Should we go?
2. Can we talk?
3. Could we have a moment alone?
4. Should we get on with it?
5. Can we go now?
6. Should we get another job?
7. Could we try to get her opinion?
8. Can we not talk about this now?
9. Should we go to the movies?
10. Could we avoid him?

Dialogue

A: Hey, could we talk?
B: Oh hi. Can we talk later? I'm on a deadline.
A: Should we make an appointment?
B: Ok. I'd just rather—could we not do this now?
A: What? I'm just asking, can we talk?
B: Should we just avoid each other?
A: What?
B: Isn't that what you're really asking?
A: Can we just take it down a notch?
B: I don't know, *can* we?

Can't You? Won't You? Don't You?

Looks Like	**Sounds Like**	**As In**
can't you	canchoo	Canchoo do it?
won't you	wonchoo	Wonchoo try?
don't you	donchoo	Donchoo want to?

Sentences

1. Can't you do it?
2. Don't you want to try?
3. Why won't you give up?
4. Can't you see it my way?
5. Won't you calm down?
6. Don't you think we should try?
7. Won't you miss him?
8. Can't you come visit again?
9. Don't you dare mention it!
10. Why can't you ever focus for a change!

Tip: Use your good judgement about this elision. It works most of the time when there's a [t] going into the word *you*. But you don't want to overdo it, and you don't want to lean into it too heavily or it can sound cheesy.

Dialogue

A: Why can't you think of anyone but yourself?
B: Why don't you make me? ("whyncha")
A: Don't you want to broaden your horizons?
B: Why can't you give me a break? I work hard.
A: Don't you start making excuses.
B: Why won't you stop accusing me?
A: I'm not accusing you. Why don't you calm down? ("whyncha")
B: Can't you … won't you …
A: What?
B: Don't you know how to finish that sentence?
A: No, I don't. Can't you put it into words?
B: Let me call you later.

Did You? Could You? Would You? Should You?

Looks Like	Sounds Like	As In
did you	dijoo	Didjoo do it?
could you	cujoo	Cujoo try?
would you	wujoo	Wujoo want to?
should you	shujoo	Shujoo go?

Sentences

1. Could you get on that?
2. Would you talk to him for me?
3. Should you take those together?
4. Did you mean that?
5. Would you mind?
6. Should you be in here *really*?
7. Did you want to ask me something?
8. Could you not?
9. Would you get out of here please?
10. Should you be on your way?

> *How do I say ...*
> really?
> ['ɪɪli]
> RILL-y
> really.

Dialogue

A: Could you ... uh ...
B: What?
A: Just ... would you mind?
B: Did you want something?
A: Just would you mind moving this?
B: Could you leave me alone, please.
A: Did you think this was just open to the public?
B: Would you please go?
A: *Did* you?
B: Did *you*?

5
CHALLENGING WORDS

These are words that don't fit into a particular category, but nevertheless get a special pronunciation in GenAm.

What, From, Of

Looks Like	Sounds Like	Does Not Resemble
what	wutt	watt
from	frumm	rom
of	uv	off

Sentences

1. What's that one of?
2. Where are you from?
3. It's from the IRS.
4. What are you thinking of?
5. What? From what?
6. Wait, watch what?
7. It's a picture of someone from here.
8. It's a rom-com from Romania.

74 Challenging Words

9. What? *What??* What???
10. Where's this rum from?

Dialogue

A: What's your name?
B: I'm _____. What's yours?
A: _____. Where are you from?
B: I'm originally from _____. Where are you from?
A: _____, originally. What?
B: What?
A: I'm asking you what. What are you thinking of?
B: Not *of* anything. Just…
A: What?
B: You're from _____, but you don't have an accent.
A: Oh. That's not what I thought you were thinking of.
B: Oh, well, what then?
A: Never mind what, that's what.

Was/Wasn't

Looks Like
was/wasn't

Sounds Like
wuzz/wuzznt

Does Not Resemble
wahz

Sentences

1. What was I saying?
2. What was that?
3. Do you know who she was?
4. I was! I swear I was!
5. Was he fuzzy?
6. He was fuzzy! He really was!
7. Well, I was, but he certainly wasn't.
8. I said I *was* buzzing the buzzer.
9. Well, your cousin was.
10. Because I was. Wasn't I?

Dialogue

A: What was I saying?
B: Actually I was talking.
A: What?
B: What? I was.
A: Wasn't I?
B: No, first she was, then I was.
A: Because I thought I was.
B: No, that was me.
A: Uh...
B: It was. Sorry, it was.
A: Because I was listening.
B: I know, I was noticing you were.
Thank you.
A: I was happy to hear your point of view.
B: Thanks, it was a good idea I had there.
A: It really was. Sorry I was interrupting.
B: It wasn't a big deal.
A: So where was I?

Actually

Looks Like
actually

Sounds Like
akshully

Does Not Resemble
aktchully or atchully

Sentences

1. I actually kind of like it.
2. Well, actually you did.
3. Are you actually going to tell me that? ("akshully gonna")
4. I think he's actually crazy, though.
5. It actually looks more like a Monet than a Renoir.
6. Actually, you're right.
7. I don't agree, actually.
8. In actuality, it's the same thing.
9. Sorry, are we actually having this conversation?
10. Right, but what did you actually say?
11. I actually tried, but he wasn't up for it.
12. Ashley's actually my best friend.

> **Tip:** Think of your nice friend Ashley, but with a K in the middle.
> "Hi, this is my friend Akshley."

Something

Looks Like
something

Sounds Like
sumpthing

Does Not Resemble
some-thing

Sentences

1. Something old, something new, something borrowed, something blue.
2. Is there something I can do for you?
3. I'm thinking of something I'd like to try.
4. It's something I cooked.
5. Could you help me with something?
6. You're making something out of nothing.
7. You gain something, you lose something.
8. That's something I can't abide.

6
INTONATION AND IDENTITY

Introduction to GenAm Intonation

The first thing you might notice about GenAm intonation, possibly to your displeasure, is how flat it seems. Where did all your expressivity go? All of a sudden, you're ironed out and slurred together.

That's partly true. If you think of the human voice as a piano, American women might speak, in a given day, on three notes. American men? Maybe one note.

Fear not. There are many ways to be expressive within those confines.

The first thing to do is master the art of stressing a word using *volume* rather than *pitch*. I don't mean you have to boom, but think of your speech as existing more horizontally than vertically. Increase the volume just a little on the stressed words, but stay more or less on the same note of your voice.

> *I have to **go** now.*
> *I **love** that part of town.*
> *You're **never** wrong.*
> *It's the same thing every **time**.*

The other thing is that, when emotional, Brits tend to bite into consonant sounds.

> ***Get* *out*!**
> *Why **do** you **keep** **going** on about it?*
> *I wish I'd never **been** **born**!*
> *You're **tearing** me **apart**, **Lisa**!*

We really hear the *g* ... *t* ... *d* ... *k* ... *b*. But Americans don't lean into consonants that way. Rather, we tend to open up the vowels and get louder.

> *Get ouuuut!*
> *Whyyyy do you keep going ooon about it?*
> *I wiiiish I'd never been boooorrrn.*
> *You're tearing me apaaarrt, Lisaaa!*

Give it a try using this passage from Mark Twain's *The Mysterious Stranger*.[1] Try keeping your pitch to 1–3 notes, and get louder on the bold words, rather than higher:

> There has never been a **just war**, never an **honorable** one—on the part of the **instigator** of the war. I can see a million years **ahead**, and this **rule** will never **change** in so many as half a dozen **instances**. The loud little **handful**—as **usual**—will shout for the **war**. The **pulpit** will—**warily** and **cautiously**—**object**—at **first**; the great, big, dull **bulk** of the **nation** will rub its sleepy **eyes** and try to make **out** why there **should** be a war, and will **say**, **earnestly** and **indignantly**, "It is **unjust** and **dishonorable**, and there is no **necessity** for it." Then the **handful** will shout **louder**. A few fair **men** on the other **side** will **argue** and reason **against** the war with **speech** and **pen**, and at **first** will have a **hearing** and be **applauded**; but it will not **last** long; those **others** will **outshout** them, and **presently** the anti-**war** audiences will thin **out** and lose **popularity**. Before **long** you will see this curious **thing**: the speakers **stoned** from the **platform**, and free **speech strangled** by hordes of furious **men** who in their secret **hearts** are

still at one with those stoned **speakers**—as **earlier**—but do not dare to **say** so. And now the whole **nation**—pulpit and **all**—will take up the **war**-cry, and shout itself **hoarse**, and **mob** any honest **man** who ventures to open his **mouth**; and **presently** such mouths will cease to **open**.

Question Intonation

This a common area of confusion. (And if you just said "area-r of confusion" in your head, go back and do the intrusive R drill in Chapter 3.) One main difference between American and British intonation is in Yes/No questions. These are questions to which you're expecting a one-word response:

*Can you **go** now?*
*Are we **there** yet?*
*Is it **hot** in here?*
*Do you want to go **out** with me on Friday?*

For these, Brits lift the pitch of the stressed word and let the rest of the phrase fall. Americans do the opposite. We drop *down* on the stressed word and lift the rest of the sentence *up*. Listen to the audio companion for the following. When you ask an *open question* (expecting an extended answer), the intonation does the reverse, going *up-down*.

Closed Questions (Yes/No)	*Open Questions (Extended Answer)*
Do you want to talk to Dad?	How's Dad?
Have you ever been to Spain?	How was your trip to Spain?
Could you see if we have any milk left?	What do we need from the store?
Do you want to?	How do you know you want to?
Were you able to hear us?	How did we sound?
Was it further than ten miles?	How far was it?
Did you watch the sunset?	What'd you think of the sunset?
Are you that guy from that movie?	What have I seen you in?
Do you want the red one?	Which one do you want?
Can we get some bottles for the road?	What do you want to have on the road?

Valley Girls and Surfer Dudes

It's extremely common for Brits and Aussies to feel less intelligent in their American accents. Sometimes, this leads to a kind of accent nihilism. Hopeless of ever finding a clear path, the actor indulges the worst stereotype of a "valley girl" or a "surfer dude." (This is nothing against valley girls and surfer dudes.)

One of the ways this tendency manifests is in up-gliding? So you sound? Like you're asking a question? When in fact it's a statement?

Simply put: don't do it. You don't have to! Instead, do the real work on finding out who *you* are in your American accent and embody that with bold sincerity and heart.

Which brings us to …

Accent as Identity

For everyone learning GenAm, there comes a time when all the technical elements are there. You're doing your R's, your A's are perfection, you're doing all your "trynas." But something's missing. You still don't feel like, well, *you*. It's somebody else's voice. Coming out of your mouth. Creepy, right?

Neuroscience confirms it. In a recent study, actors were put in an MRI machine and asked to speak first as themselves, then as a character, and finally as themselves using a foreign accent. Guess what? The parts of the brain that activate when playing a character also light up when doing an accent, even when speaking as yourself. Similarly, the parts of the brain that regulate self-processing (the story you tell yourself about yourself) are de-activated. That means you quite literally feel like a different person, just by changing the way you speak.[2]

This obviously poses challenges for acting in your American accent. After all, in order to act well, you must make deep and specific use of yourself. What's to be done if the accent quite literally turns your "self" off?

The answer, as I see it, is to find a version of yourself that comes out when you speak this way. It's not the you of your childhood, exactly, but it is a character so specifically rooted in your personality and associations, it still allows you access to yourself. Imagine putting on a pair of thigh-high patent leather boots and going for a walk. Are you still you? Yes, but a different version of yourself. Now change out the boots for bare feet. Or roller skates. Who are you now? Still you, but a little bit different. That's how I see an accent: a tool to ignite and release a new part of yourself.

So, who do you get to be in your American accent? Let's find out.

What Are Your Stereotypes?

> *I think we're raised to have a slight snobbishness towards how Americans speak.*
>
> —Polly McKie, actor from Glasgow

Many Brits and Aussies strongly dislike American accents. Ask yourself if this is the case for you, and be honest. Do you think American accents make people sound dumb? Uneducated? Grating? Annoying? Take a moment and think of every single negative stereotype you have. Get it all out. I've included some of the more common words my clients come up with for inspiration.

obnoxious   grating   annoying   nasal   whiny   spoiled   too loud   dumb stupid   uneducated   low-class   rude   brassy   entitled   superficial   fake chipper   smug   macho   like a bimbo   idiotic   boring   monotone unintelligible   unexpressive   lazy   unsophisticated   like John Wayne like "The Nanny"   like a valley girl

Next, you'll work to develop a positive impression of who you can be in *your* American accent. But for now, it's important to confront these stereotypes, so you know where you're starting from.

"When I Speak This Way ..."[3]

> *The most challenging thing about speaking GenAm is making it sound like your own voice. That's always the struggle.*
>
> —Robert Spence, actor from Reading

Get a pen and paper. Sit quietly, and get into the mindset of your American accent. Maybe say a few words to warm up. Then, in GenAm, say aloud the following:

When I speak this way, I am …

And say whatever words come to mind. More than likely, these may be words like *foolish*, *an idiot*, *fake*, etc. Push past that and see if you can get to any words that are positive. If you're still stuck, try these prompts:

When I speak this way, I am more …
When I speak this way, I am less …

Try to stay away from unconsciously changing the wording to "When I speak this way I *feel* …" Somehow, that's more temporary. We're after who you *are* in this accent.

Write down as many words as come to mind. Though no two people have ever come up with the same list, here are some common favorites:

laid-back   cool   versatile   powerful   from here   global   a shapeshifter youthful   wide/big   brassy   a little bossy   worthy   disciplined   aware conscientious   focused   magic   pointed   generous   large and in charge

Now, narrow it down to three. Your favorite three that crackle inside you and feel just right. Ideally, they should be different qualities—not synonyms. Then, add your name.

My name is Amanda, and when I speak this way, I am cool, articulate, and razor-sharp.

Think of it as your personal Believe-In-Your-Accent mantra.

If you're really stuck, and you can only seem to come up with negative words, there are ways to work with that. Here are some common negative words and ways you can turn them into positives:

self-conscious	...	*aware, conscientious, disciplined*
foolish	...	*bold, brave, risk-taking*
a fraud	...	*versatile, a shapeshifter, magical*
stupid	...	*laid-back, wide open, innocent, young*
small	...	*contained, focused, pointed, on-point*
obnoxious	...	*in the middle of it, outgoing, extroverted*
low class	...	*unpretentious, cool*
smug	...	*powerful, skilled, a pro, fierce*
unexpressive	...	*subtle, deep, mysterious, stoic*
lazy	...	*laid-back, effortless, at ease, easygoing*

You get the picture. It might seem a little silly at first, but keep at it. It's worth it. Here are some of my favorites from clients:

My name is Sarah, and when I speak this way, I am cool, global, and in the middle of it.

My name is John, and when I speak this way, I am large, commanding, and sly.

My name is Frank, and when I speak this way, I am laid-back, clear, and generous.

My name is Gretchen, and when I speak this way, I am feisty, bold, and no-nonsense.

My name is Lucas, and when I speak this way, I am self-aware, focused, and a little bossy.

"Where Are You From?"

In your GenAm survival kit, it's essential to address this question, especially if you're an actor living and working in the US. Nothing strikes more anxiety and frustration into the hearts of my clients than this seemingly innocent inquiry. Here's how it usually plays out:

You: Hi, I'm John. Nice to meet you.
Them: Nice to meet you. Thanks for coming in to audition.
You: Thanks for having me.
Them: So, where are you from?
You: [silently fuming] Erm ... England.

You immediately think you've failed at your accent. You've been exposed. Found out. You've got to reframe this. Here are some reasons a stranger might ask you where you're from:

1. They're making small talk, and it's a safe opener.
2. They think you're great, and they're wondering why they haven't met you before.
3. You look like someone they went to high school with.
4. They're curious about the origins of your last name.
5. They're casting something else that requires a certain ethnic background, and they're wondering if you're right for that.
6. You seem too cool/exotic/mysterious/charming to be from around here.
7. They detect a hint of an accent and want to show off how good their ear is.

Let's discuss #7. Here's the thing with speaking in your American accent to a group of Americans: if your native accent slips in a little bit, Americans don't hear a *bad American accent*. They hear a *light foreign accent*. In your head, *you* hear a screaming gremlin, but we don't hear that gremlin. We just hear what sounds to us like neutral words. So, if they detect a bit of an accent, keep in mind that's all it is. They hear a slight version of your native accent, they don't hear the massive, brave attempt at American you know you're doing.

And, by the way, here's a great answer to that question:

> *I'm originally from Australia.*

Somehow that word "originally" is magic here. It gives you privacy, a little distance. It's vague enough to mean you could have come here as a child, yet it's accurate enough to be the truth. It's empowering. It means, I'm from there. Now I'm here. Nice to meet you.

Refining Your GenAm

Congratulations! You've done the lion's share of work on your American accent. Now, you have a new tool to play with that will hopefully open some doors and give you confidence. Here are some tips for refining your sound to match your type.

First, find a native speaker model. This could be an actor or other public figure who has footage online that you can refer to. Your model should be the same gender and ethnicity as you, and roughly your age. If you choose an actor, make sure you're watching interviews and not just scripted material. If you choose a politician or public speaker, look for footage where they speak off-the-cuff. Find the most natural-sounding samples you can.

Here are some good GenAm models (by no means exhaustive), organized by ethnicity.

African-American

>Oprah Winfrey
>Michelle Obama
>Barack Obama
>Kamala Harris
>Viola Davis
>Laurence Fishburne
>Halle Berry
>Kerry Washington
>Cuba Gooding, Jr.
>Gabrielle Union
>Denzel Washington
>Forest Whitaker
>Sterling K. Brown

(Black actors might also want to add African-American Vernacular English (AAVE) to their arsenal. There are videos online, and Jim Johnson has a tutorial available at accenthelp.org.)

Asian-American

>Lucy Liu
>Andrew Yang
>Randall Park

Margaret Cho
B.D. Wong
Ali Wong
Constance Wu

South Asian-American

Manish Dayal
Tiya Sircar
Parvesh Cheena
Aziz Ansari
Mindy Kaling

Caucasian

Scarlett Johansson
Jennifer Lawrence
Jodie Foster
Leonardo DiCaprio
Tom Hanks
Jack Quaid
Edward Norton
Maggie Gyllenhaal
Peter Dinklage
Lizzy Caplan
Allison Janney
Elizabeth Marvel

Latinx

Oscar Isaac
Eva Longoria
Pedro Pascal
Gina Rodriguez
Diane Guerrero
America Ferrera
Ryan Guzman

Gina Torres
George Lopez
Julián Castro
Alexandria Ocasio-Cortez

Middle Eastern-American

Tony Shalhoub
Rami Malek
Omar Metwally
Gigi Hadid
Hala Gorani

Hunt around for a few of your own. It's important to find a voice you personally like and connect to. Once you've found your person, play their audio and try shadowing them with your voice—imitate their intonation as they speak, trailing just behind them. Notice what strikes you. Do they do the GenAm sounds you've learned so far? And what might be the differences?

Use their sound not as a target to rigidly mimic, but as an offering—a suggestion. Always check in with your "When I speak this way, I am …" phrase, and change your model as needed. Then ride the river of their voice back to your own.

Notes

1 Twain, Mark. (2006). *The Mysterious Stranger*. Urbana, Illinois: Project Gutenberg. Retrieved December 10, 2019, from www.gutenberg.org/ebooks/19033.
2 Brown S, Cockett P, Yuan Y. 2019. The neuroscience of Romeo and Juliet: an fMRI study of acting. *R. Soc. Open Sci*. 6: 181908. 10.1098/rsos .181908
3 This section is adapted from my training with Jan Gist.

APPENDIX

In Their Own Words: Actors on Acting in GenAm

Here is some insight and inspiration from a few of the Aussies and Brits I've worked with.

Michael Dale, *NYC via London*
"My tip would be to practice every day and use it as often as possible in everyday communication. My breakthrough moment was booking a play that required an American accent. I knew that the audition must have gone well enough for them to book me."

Laura Hooper, *NYC via Maidenhead*
"My biggest challenge was having the confidence to go into an audition speaking it and remembering how to say 'February.' I had a breakthrough when I'd been on a film set for 2 days playing a cop speaking GenAm from sunrise to sunset. When we wrapped, I broke it and spoke in my native accent and the sound guys (who were taking my mic off) freaked out and started calling the crew over. No one could tell I wasn't American! My advice is to practice speaking it in shops, read this book, take a class. And I always say if asked in an audition, 'I am originally from London but I've lived in New York

for 8 years now.' It helps eradicate the imposter syndrome if you are asked where you come from."

Polly McKie, *NYC via Glasgow*
"Unlike learning another language, GenAm involves 'unlearning' how we've been speaking all our lives. I think we're also raised to have a slight snobbishness towards how Americans speak. So I feel my family and friends would mock me for saying *tomayto*, not *tomahto*, *Bayzil*, *aluminum*, etc. Early on in the process, a huge help for me was to practice out in the real world with strangers. We had chatted about how I felt it was difficult to practice with people I knew because it felt so fake. Now, I don't even notice I'm doing it in diners, cabs, etc."

Victoria Hill, *NYC and Sydney via Adelaide*
"The most challenging thing is speaking GenAm with other Americans. Self-consciousness clicks in a way I have not experienced in other accents, or indeed other USA dialects. My advice would be to immerse yourself and speak American in coffee shops, in cabs, with strangers, etc. Also find an American teacher if you can. I think working with an Aussie teaching GenAm to other Aussies is one step too removed for me personally."

Lisa Donmall-Reeve, *NYC via London*
"The most challenging thing is trying to let the acting still be present and real whilst nailing the accent—not totally focusing on just the accent."

Robert Spence, *NYC via Reading, Berkshire*
"Don't do your GenAm accent for friends as a party trick! Friends will always ask me to 'do my American accent' because they think it's funny to hear me speak differently. It's not worth feeling self-conscious about something that I'm already self-conscious about! Better to keep it for the professional arena when needed. Also, like many actors, I've worked in restaurants and that's a great opportunity to practice with strangers."

Appendix

Charles Nassif, *NYC via Sydney*
"Knowing the rules and how they apply is the challenge. Once you conquer these, you have it! Practice. Go to classes and learn from others. Learn the rules. It will take some time, but once mastered, it is so empowering."

Zoë Watkins, *NYC via Welwyn Garden City, Hertfordshire*
"For me, it was psychological – I felt so fake and out of 'my truth' that I had no confidence in myself, so that when people inevitably questioned it I lost even more confidence. I think the persistent work is the thing and that builds confidence! So just keep at it. Relax. Work hard at not working hard!"

Oliver Thornton, *NYC via Wales and London*
"I had used an American accent whilst acting on the West End and thought it was 'generally good enough.' Within weeks of moving to the US, it became apparent that a 'general' ability to do an accent is nowhere near good enough when trying to pass in the country of origin, and my confidence began to crumble. At that point, I didn't even want to express myself in my own accent. Speaking became a horrible prospect because either I was in my own British accent and Americans would innocently draw attention to it, or I'd be practicing my American, and this garnered equal attention.

The difference between the small amount of accent training I received throughout my dramatic training in the UK and passing as native in front of an American audience is vast. An accent is so much more than just sounds, it's having the confidence to embody someone else's childhood, their culture, a national identity and an attitude which is born of their life experiences. If it isn't integral it becomes a perceptible 'layer' which you are adding to the character.

Gaining the confidence to retain the essence of who I am but rediscovering a new 'version' of myself began with GenAm classes. I gave myself permission to explore who I am in the American accent. This didn't mean that I was becoming two people, but I definitely had to take a journey to come back to myself and allow myself to 'be' in an accent which wasn't my own.

My advice would be to take it seriously. I'm embarrassed to admit that working on a passable accent was an afterthought prior to moving to the States. I just didn't appreciate how much we communicate through an accent. How the specific combination of sounds that leave our mouths work on an emotional level for both speaker, and listener. The ability to 'blend' might seem counterintuitive in a profession which thrives on one's ability to stand out, but I truly believe the study of the American accent is one of the greatest gifts any young actor could give themselves. It's really hard to speak with any kind of truth when you're catching every word that comes out of your mouth."

Nathan Spiteri, *NYC via Canberra*
"The best part is going to auditions with my GenAm accent, doing the audition, then speaking with my Aussie accent once I'm done and casting having no idea I'm not American. You might feel funny and self-conscious, but you will get it. Keep at it. The more you practice and speak with the accent in your everyday life, the easier it will get."

For Product Safety Concerns and Information please contact our EU
representative GPSR@taylorandfrancis.com
Taylor & Francis Verlag GmbH, Kaufingerstraße 24, 80331 München, Germany

www.ingramcontent.com/pod-product-compliance
Lightning Source LLC
Chambersburg PA
CBHW051529230426
43668CB00012B/1792